OPEN CONCEPT APARTMENTS

OPEN CONCEPT APARTMENTS

Francesc Zamora Mola

HARPER
DESIGN
An Imprint of HarperCollins Publishers

HarperCollins books may be purchased for educational, business, or sales promotional use.
For information, please email Special Markets Department at SPsales@harpercollins.com.

First published in 2018 by:
Harper Design
An Imprint of HarperCollins*Publishers*
195 Broadway
New York, NY 10007
Tel.: (212) 207-7000
Fax: (855) 746-6023
harperdesign@harpercollins.com
www.hc.com

Distributed throughout the world by:
HarperCollins*Publishers*
195 Broadway
New York, NY 10007

Editorial coordinator: Claudia Martínez Alonso
Art director: Mireia Casanovas Soley
Editor and texts: Francesc Zamora Mola
Layout: Cristina Simó Perales

ISBN 978-0-06-284060-8

Library of Congress Control Number: 2017963488

Printed in China
First printing, 2018

6   INTRODUCTION
8   FLOUR MILL LOFT
24 RENOVATED TRIBECA PENTHOUSE
34 A.R. APARTMENT
48 HUDSON LOFT
60 EAST 70TH STREET DUPLEX
70 SKY AND SPACE
80 ATTIC CONVERSION
92 APARTMENT COMBINATION AND TOTAL REMODEL
106 ART COLLECTOR'S LOFT
116 LA CASA OF PAUL AND SIGI
126 FIFTH AVENUE RESIDENCE
142 LAUSANNE
158 FLATIRON LOFT MEETS BALI
170 EAST 90TH STREET APARTMENT
180 GREENWICH VILLAGE APARTMENT COMBINATION
192 MARINE LOFT
204 UPPER EAST SIDE APARTMENT COMBINATION
214 EAST 69TH STREET APARTMENT
228 BEATTY STREET LOFT
240 WEST 67TH STREET RESIDENCE
252 CONTEMPORARY LOFT
266 PREWAR UPPER EAST SIDE RENOVATION
276 CHIADO APARTMENT
284 HARRISON AVENUE APARTMENT
294 WEISEL APARTMENT
306 BONDI APARTMENT
322 QUEEN STREET APARTMENT
334 PETROLEUM APARTMENT
348 OVERLAP
362 GALLERY LOFT APARTMENT
376 ART AND LIGHT
388 POTTS POINT APARTMENT
400 FORMER CARETAKER'S APARTMENT
416 TRAMA
428 MIDTOWN WEST
436 RF HOME
448 EFFICIENT LIVING
456 EAST VILLAGE STUDIO
468 CAMINHA APARTMENT

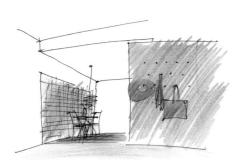

Introduction

Opening up an apartment's floor plan appears to be a desirable home improvement, one that resolves the lack of space and promotes a more casual, family-friendly lifestyle. Open plans seem to have become the "default" layout in both newly designed and refurbished apartments. Could the reason be that they have become a trend or perhaps they are the reflection of a lifestyle that calls for convenience and sociability?

These changes might explain how the kitchen, which for a long time has occupied a separate space in the home, has become the epicenter of family life and entertainment. It shares a large open space with the living and dining areas. Combining these spaces surely makes sense when dealing with limited space. If we think about it, walls, doors, and hallways can take up a considerable amount of floor area. With fewer walls, open floor plans feel larger, allow for more natural lighting, and promote flexible use of space, adapting to the users' changing needs and living patterns.

This book is a compilation of such cases, where outdated and over-compartmentalized apartments are opened up to facilitate fluid circulation between different parts of the home, to promote social interaction, and to bring natural lighting from the peripheral areas with windows and outdoor spaces deeper into the apartment.

Beginning with an overview of the existing conditions and a wish list of changes, architects, interior designers, and owners bring in their own experiences to point out the challenges faced during remodeling processes, for instance, code issues, structural upgrading, pipework changes, and the inability to fully satisfy the owners' requirements due to an inadequate budget. Despite the difficulties, the projects included in this book demonstrate that these challenges can be overcome with ingenious design solutions.

FLOUR MILL LOFT

3,000 sq. ft.

Denver, Colorado, United States

STUDIO GILD
Photos © David Lauer

Design team: **Jennie Bishop, Kristen Ekeland, and Melissa Benham**

www.studiogild.com

> RECONFIGURE THE CORE OF THE LOFT, COMPRISING THE KITCHEN, GUEST BATHROOM, AND LAUNDRY ROOM

> REMODEL MASTER BATHROOM AND MASTER CLOSET

> REFURBISH FIREPLACE

THIS LOFT IS LOCATED ON THE FIFTH FLOOR OF A SIX-STORY FORMER FLOUR MILL. THE BUILDING WAS BUILT IN THE 1920s. IT WAS ABANDONED AT SOME POINT IN THE 1950s. IN THE 1990s, UNDER THREAT OF DEMOLITION, THE BUILDING WAS REFURBISHED FOR RESIDENTIAL USE, AND IS NOW ON THE NATIONAL REGISTER OF HISTORIC PLACES.

"This project began, primarily, as a full furnishing project with very few architectural enhancements included in our scope of work. The entire process, from conception to end of construction, took nearly a year. Once the last piece of furniture was in place, the client decided it was time to renovate the kitchen and two full bathrooms. This is how phase two got under way. We collaborated with Denver-based architect Robb Studio to reconfigure the core of the loft, which comprises the kitchen, guest bathroom, and laundry room. Also, the master bathroom and a fireplace found new life in this phase.

"The owner enjoyed participating in the process, researching the latest technologies and integrating them into the design of the space when possible. He also enjoyed investigating the best creative solutions when challenges arose. This type of collaboration made the process very inspiring.

"Because our aesthetics meshed so well, the client gave us carte blanche to choose furniture and help design custom millwork pieces."

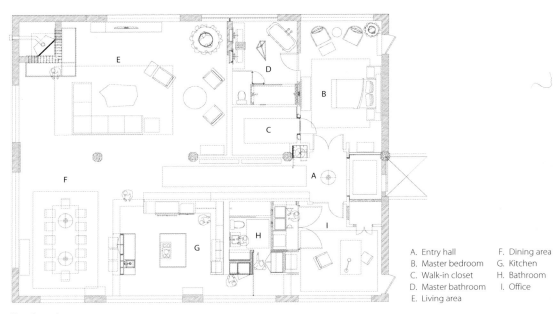

New floor plan

A. Entry hall   F. Dining area
B. Master bedroom   G. Kitchen
C. Walk-in closet   H. Bathroom
D. Master bathroom   I. Office
E. Living area

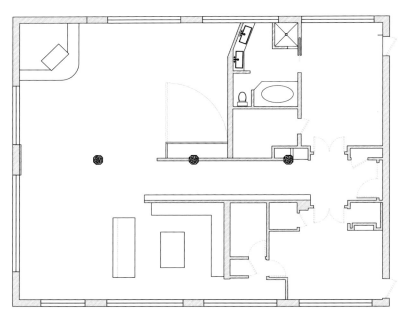

Existing floor plan

GALLERY HALL   FOYER

Elevation at gallery hall west and foyer west

The imposing La Cage bronze chandelier by Hudson Furniture brightens the entry, a tall and narrow passage flanked with custom dark aniline-dyed ash bookcases by Newell Design.

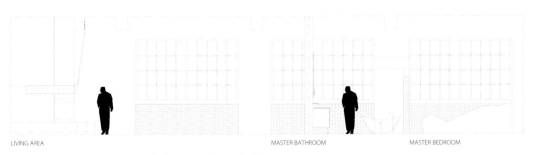

LIVING AREA

MASTER BATHROOM

MASTER BEDROOM

West elevation at living area, master bathroom, and master bedroom

The loft retains the original oak flooring, which was refinished in a soft gray tone to create warmth and to harmonize with the concrete columns and ceiling. This combination provides a homogeneous setting, where furniture and artwork throughout take center stage.

The finished space showcases
architectural details crafted with
honest materials amid antique graphic
rugs and mid-century vintage finds,
each full of character and history.

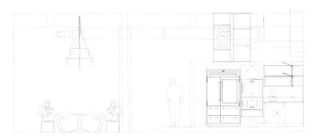

West elevation at kitchen

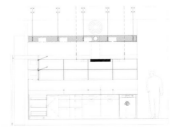

North elevation at kitchen

Close to the wall with tall windows, the kitchen receives abundant natural light. Its design, in line with the industrial character of the loft, features clean lines and sleek surfaces. The cabinetry, made of stained oak and perforated metal panels, is paired with quartzite countertops.

The master bedroom and bathroom
are located off to one side of the
entry hall, across from the office,
separate from the vast open plan
living area. The proportions of these
private zones are more intimate, but
the design maintains the industrial
character of the loft, highlighting
exposed HVAC ducting and steel
sash windows.

all is
vanity

South elevation at guest bathroom

Enhanced material palette used
throughout the loft's remodel is more
evident in areas such as the kitchen
and the bathrooms, where the design
was taken to a high level of detail.

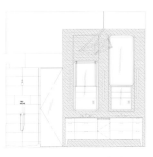

South elevation at master bathroom

Credits

Architect: Robb Studio
www.robbstudio.com

Interior Designer: Studio Gild
www.studiogild.com

Appliances and Materials

Appliances: Gaggenau and Sub-Zero
Bathroom fixtures: Vintage claw-foot tub with Grohe fixtures
Bathroom vanity: Custom Shou Sugi Ban with 6-inch carved marble slab sink
Bathroom light fixtures: Bec Brittain and Michael Anastassiades
Dining area furniture: BDDW massive custom chainsaw-charred walnut and bronze wishbone table; chairs by Christian Liaigre and Mark Albrecht Studio; and custom light fixture by Bowles and Linares.
Living area furniture: Poliform Shangai sectional on a vintage rug from Oscar Isberian Rugs; vintage and custom pieces from Newell Design, Milo Baughman, Blackman Cruz, and Pierre Anthony Galleries. Custom island barstools; entry hall's La Cage chandelier by Hudson Furniture. Leather, suede, horsehair, burl wood, and aged wool dominate the living room.
Kitchen cabinetry: Custom oak and metal by EKD
Kitchen countertops: Quartzite and stainless steel
Kitchen fixtures: Kallista

RENOVATED TRIBECA PENTHOUSE

3,000 sq. ft.

New York, New York, United States

—

THE TURETT COLLABORATIVE

Photos © The Turett Collaborative

Designer: Wayne Turett, RA, LEED

www.turettarch.com

> MODERNIZE THE FLOOR PLAN

> MAKE USE OF AMPLE LIGHT AND EXISTING
  OVERSIZED WINDOWS

> OPEN UP THE KITCHEN TO THE LIVING AND
  DINING AREAS

PERCHED HIGH ABOVE THE TRIBECA NEIGHBORHOOD, THIS DUPLEX PENTHOUSE BRINGS TOGETHER ARCHITECTURAL HERITAGE AND CONTEMPORARY COMFORT.

"The duplex had original features we wanted to preserve, but at the same time we wanted to create a living environment that was contemporary. With that in mind, our goal was to create a cohesive whole, rather than a composition of old and new parts.

"Multiple skylights and windows on three sides facing north, east, and south, offering sweeping views, ensure that this penthouse receives abundant natural light. The existing windows are very distinctive. They are oversized, and the detailing makes a strong design statement. It was clear to us that we had to incorporate them into our design.

"The clients wanted to keep all finishes on the materials neutral, so, as they put it: 'we wouldn't get tired of them too soon with a two-bedroom apartment and a growing family.'"

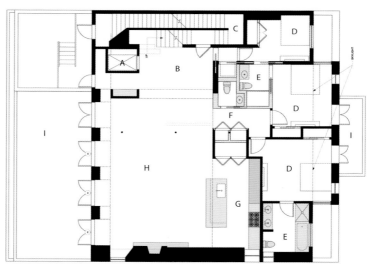

New floor plan

The renovation of the penthouse encompasses updates mainly on the lower level. The private elevator entrance gives way to the open plan, where a spacious living, dining, and kitchen area leads out to a massive private deck promoting a contemporary lifestyle.

A. Elevator
B. Entry hall
C. Staircase
D. Bedroom
E. Bathroom
F. Hall
G. Kitchen
H. Living/dining area
I. Terrace

The penthouse has wide white oak plank flooring, distinctive oversized windows, and glass doors that reinforce the open character of the spaces. In the living and dining area, a wood burning fireplace and large TV screen are integrated into a dark-stained wood feature wall that sets the tone for the entire home.

The master suite is on its own floor with a generously sized walk-in closet, a separate sauna and steam room, and two terraces.

The master bedroom and bathroom
are light-filled and comfortable. They
offer an atmosphere of personal
indulgence and a true spa experience.

Credits

Architect: The Turett Collaborative
www.turettarch.com

Appliances and Materials

Appliances: Refrigerator by Sub-Zero; dishwasher, wall oven, wall steam oven, convection oven, microwave, and built-in coffee maker by Gaggenau
Bathroom: Teak wood flooring by TerraMai
Master bathroom: "Glacier White" countertop by Corian; "Novelda Cream" limestone walls, Artemide light fixtures

Bathroom walls: Athens silver cream marble tile from Ann Sacks, Bianco Dolomiti marble countertops and tub deck, Duravit toilets, Hansgrohe fixtures and custom vanities.
Dining area light: Apparatus
Door hardware: Omnia
Kitchen cabinetry: Snaidero
Kitchen countertop: Corian

Kitchen fixtures: Sink by Kallista and faucet by Dornbracht
Kitchen lighting: Plug
Wood floors: Town and Country flooring

A.R. APARTMENT

3,488 sq. ft.

São Paulo, Brazil

ROCCO ARQUITETOS

Photos © Ana Mello

Design team: Giancarlo Rocco, Ana Lúcia
Pasquali Rocco, and Simone Ferreira

www.roccoarquitetos.com.br

> OPEN UP THE UPPER FLOOR TO CREATE AN
EXPANSIVE LIVING AREA SUITABLE FOR
ENTERTAINING

> OPTIMIZE ACCESS TO TERRACE

> CREATE A FLEXIBLE LAYOUT FACILITATED BY
LARGE SLIDING DOORS

THE NEW DESIGN OF THE UPPER LEVEL IN THIS DUPLEX APARTMENT TURNS A POORLY PLANNED ROOM ORGANIZATION INTO A FLUID SEQUENCE OF SPACES FOR ENTERTAINING.

"The apartment is a duplex with the lower floor accommodating the living and dining areas, the kitchen, and the bedrooms. Access to the apartment is on this floor, but our scope of work was centered on the upper level. Its original layout didn't take full advantage of its spatial and functional possibilities.

"With the new configuration, the upper floor has a roomy open space with a gourmet kitchen and a generous dining counter. It also has a TV space, which can be closed off or be an extension of the open space whenever needed. The use of cement flooring, wood, steel, and glass created a clean, natural, and relaxed environment.

"This floor has access to a spacious terrace. This outdoor space can be an extension of the living area, allowing large gatherings to spill out, or can also be a desirable private outdoor retreat perched in the sky."

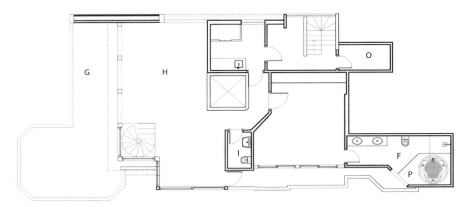

Existing upper floor plan

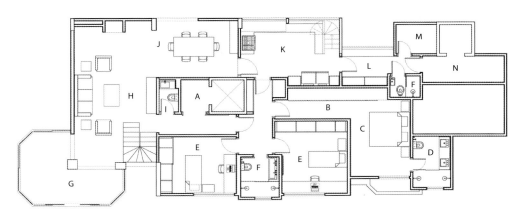

Existing lower floor plan

A. Elevator lobby
B. Dressing area
C. Master bedroom
D. Master bathroom
E. Bedroom
F. Bathroom
G. Terrace
H. Living area

I. Powder room
J. Dining area
K. Kitchen
L. Pantry
M. Maid's room
N. Service elevator lobby
O. Storage
P. Sauna

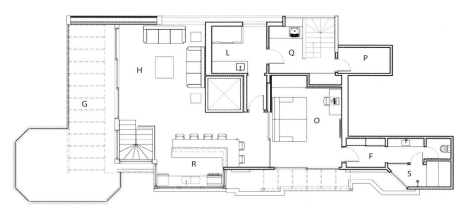

New upper floor plan

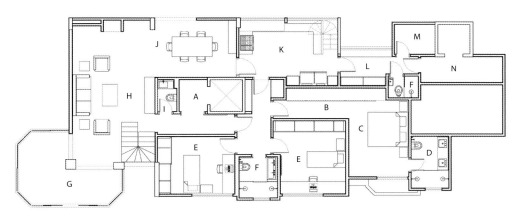

New lower floor plan

A. Elevator lobby
B. Dressing area
C. Master bedroom
D. Master bathroom
E. Bedroom
F. Bathroom
G. Terrace
H. Living area
I. Powder room
J. Dining area

K. Kitchen
L. Pantry
M. Maid's room
N. Service elevator lobby
O. Media room
P. Storage
Q. Laundry room
R. Gourmet kitchen
S. Sauna

The most significant changes took place on the top floor where various walls were knocked down to create a spacious living area.

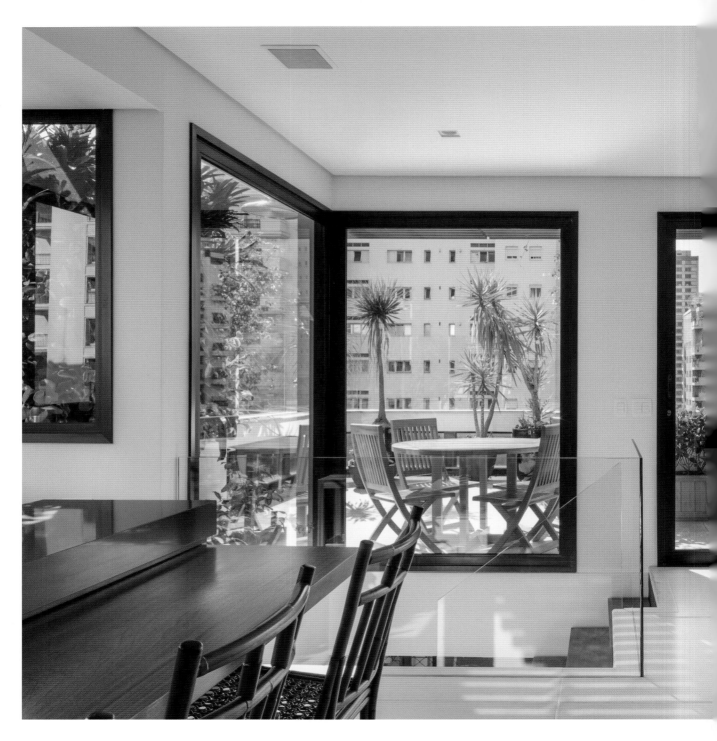

The gourmet kitchen on the upper floor was specifically designed for entertaining. The former enclosed kitchen with limited functionality was transformed into a hub around which family and guests gather for quality time.

The media room was conceived as a flexible space. This design is optimized by means of two oversized pocket doors, which can remain closed to maintain a separate area or be opened, allowing a party to spill into the space.

A sculptural staircase was made with a 3/8" thick steel plate with cumaru wood treads to match all the other wood surfaces in the apartment. Expanded wire mesh guardrails enhance the lightweight design of the staircase.

Because cumaru is a rot resistant
wood, it was also used on the terrace.
A glass roof over a wood pergola
keeps the terrace dry and usable
even on rainy days. All the aluminum
guardrails were replaced by frameless
glass to increase the sense of
lightness and transparency.

Credits

Architect: Giancarlo Rocco / Rocco Arquitetos
www.roccoarquitetos.com.br

General contractor: Ciampolini Rocco

**Landscape designer:
Teodoro Marques da Costa**

Appliances and Materials

Floors: Polished concrete (indoors and outdoors).
Gourmet kitchen countertop:
"Cemento Spa" by Silestone

HUDSON LOFT

3,000 sq. ft.

New York, New York, United States

**SCHAPPACHERWHITE
ARCHITECTURE DPC**

Photos © Jason Lindberg

Design team: **Steve Schappacher**, partner;
Rhea White, partner; and **Heather Mangrum**,
project designer

www.schappacherwhite.com

> COMBINE TWO EXITING LOFTS INTO ONE
  SINGLE HOME

> FLEXIBLE DESIGN SUITABLE FOR FAMILY
  LIVING AND ENTERTAINING

> HIGHLIGHT THE ARCHITECTURAL CHARACTER
  OF THE ORIGINAL SPACES

THIS NEWLY REMODELED LOFT EXHIBITS BEAUTY AND CHARACTER WITH MATERIALS THAT BEAR THE PATINA OF AGE.

"Located in the former American Express warehouse building in Tribeca, two lofts were combined to create ample new living space. The clients lived in the building for years before purchasing the second neighboring loft for their growing family.

"Tribeca is known for its large loft spaces and is a short walk to Wall Street, both of which are appealing to the owners.

"The clients and the architects wanted to reference the history of the neighborhood, the building, and existing details of the interior, while maintaining an open loft feeling that was flexible in the way it could be used. The design allows for modifiable use of the space, suitable for both family living and entertaining. Similarly, the bedrooms can spill into adjacent public areas, but are also appointed with the needed privacy. The materials allow for use and wear, as it is a family home that is meant to be used and enjoyed."

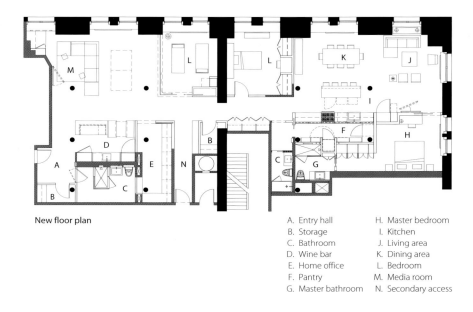

New floor plan

A. Entry hall
B. Storage
C. Bathroom
D. Wine bar
E. Home office
F. Pantry
G. Master bathroom

H. Master bedroom
I. Kitchen
J. Living area
K. Dining area
L. Bedroom
M. Media room
N. Secondary access

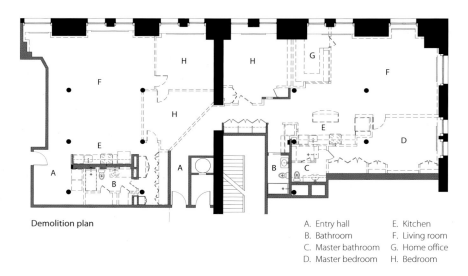

Demolition plan

A. Entry hall
B. Bathroom
C. Master bathroom
D. Master bedroom

E. Kitchen
F. Living room
G. Home office
H. Bedroom

The two lofts were combined into a
larger home that is as comfortable for
family life as it is for gatherings.

Fumed oak was used as flooring material and on the front of the kitchen island.

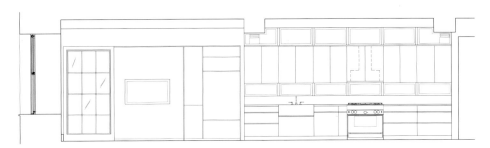

Elevation at kitchen

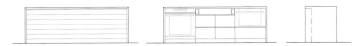

Elevation at kitchen island

The kitchen incorporates custom steel pivot windows that open to the pantry, providing this room with ventilation and natural light. This is a play on kitchen windows typically looking out onto a garden.

The design evolved from the
warehouse's history, materials,
and forms of the existing spaces.

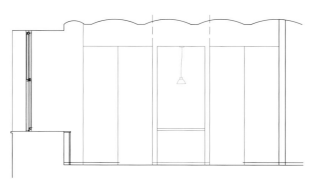

Elevation at bedroom

Translucent fiberglass panels were also used in doors and partitions to allow light to filter into adjoining spaces.

The loft design was created with a thoughtful and streamlined approach, including high quality materials and complete customization. This steel shower enclosure, designed by SchappacherWhite Architecture and fabricated by Gunnar Design, is an example of the work that can set a project apart.

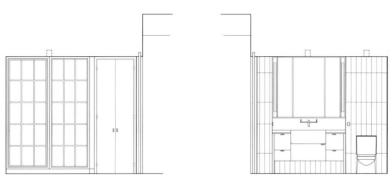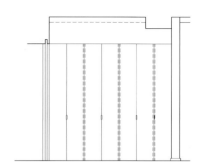

Elevation at master bathroom

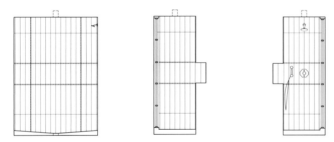

Elevations at master bathroom shower

Credits

Architect:
SchappacherWhite Architecture DPC
www.schappacherwhite.com

Engineer:
Richard Lemansky / RHL Engineering

General contractor:
ZT Maximum Construction

Metal design and fabrication:
Gunnar Design
www.gunnardesign.com

Appliances and Materials

Art at dining room: Bill Sullivan
Custom cabinetry: ZT Max
Construction
Dining room credenza: BDDW
Encaustic wallpaper: "Evergreen
Studio" by Studio B
Floors: Fumed white oak by ZT Max
Construction
Lighting: O'Lampia Studio and Urban
Electric

Plumbing fixtures: Metropolitan
Home Hardware & Bath
Walls: Paint and chemically treated steel

EAST 70TH STREET DUPLEX

3,000 sq. ft.

New York, New York, United States

———

S4ARCHITECTURE
Photos © Beatrice Pediconi

Design team: Michele Busiri-Vici and Clementina Ruggieri, architects; Annie Mennes, project manager

www.space4architecture.com

> DESIGN A SPACE THAT CAN COMFORTABLY ACCOMMODATE A FAMILY OF EIGHT

> CREATE A SENSE OF OPENNESS IN THE LIVING AREAS AND DEVISE COMPACT BEDROOMS AND BATHROOMS

THIS DUPLEX, REDESIGNED BY S4ARCHITECTURE FOR A FAMILY OF EIGHT, ACHIEVES A REMARKABLE SENSE OF SPACIOUSNESS AND FLOW.

"We were charged with designing a home that could accommodate a family of eight in a New York City duplex. From the beginning, our concept was to dedicate openness to the common areas and create compact, yet comfortable, bedrooms and bathrooms.

"The staircase was the one critical element that could either enhance the open and airy feel or ruin the entire concept. The goal was to make it a focal point without causing obstruction. Basically, it had to live up to the remarkable spatial quality of the apartment duplex.

"Fortunately, it all worked out and the result couldn't have been more stunning. We created a cantilevered open staircase that is elegant and airy. It connects the two levels, which are equally as inviting and spacious."

New upper floor plan

New lower floor plan

A. Entry hall
B. Kitchen and breakfast nook
C. Living/dining area
D. Office
E. Master bedroom
F. Master closet
G. Master bathroom – hers
H. Master bathroom – his
I. Maid's room
J. Maid's bathroom and laundry room
K. Powder room
L. Bedroom
M. Mechanical room
N. Bathroom
O. Media room
P. Storage

The custom white kitchen with Corian island merges with the luminous surrounding space, creating an effect of seamless continuity. The monochromatic color scheme serves as backdrop for an extensive contemporary art collection.

The stair treads up to the second level
cantilever from a steel plate that is
concealed behind the plasterboard
wall. The floating effect contributes to
the airy atmosphere of the home.

The master bedroom is a soothing
retreat of white and soft textures,
offset by the dark hardwood flooring.

Credits

Architect: S4ARCHITECTURE
www.space4architecture.com

General contractor: Signature

Appliances and Materials

Appliances: Gaggenau and Miele
Carpentry: Custom millwork
Floors: White oak with custom
stain, poured-in-place concrete in
bathrooms
Lighting: Deltalight, Flos, Artemide,
and Alinea
Plumbing fixtures: Duravit,
Dornbracht, and Laufen

Walls: Level 5 skim coat, painted
white; custom-colored plaster and
glass tiles (bathrooms only)

SKY AND SPACE

3,000 sq. ft.

New York, New York, United States

———

ANDREW MIKHAEL ARCHITECT

Photos © Jeffrey Kilmer

Designer: Andrew Mikhael Architect

www.andrewmikhael.com

> **COMBINE THREE ADJACENT APARTMENTS**

> **CAPITALIZE ON EXPOSURES AND VIEWS**

OPEN LOFT WITH STUNNING HUDSON RIVER VIEWS

"Located at the western edge of midtown New York, our client purchased three two-bedroom apartments and a 20-foot stretch of hallway between apartments. Our call to action was to integrate these spaces into a grand, flowing home that takes advantage of the surrounding views, while providing the bedrooms with privacy.

"Combining apartments is one of the most creative ways of upsizing in a city. You get to stay in the same neighborhood and design a home that suits your needs as opposed to having to choose from what is on the market.

"Thinking of the Japanese concept of integrating natural elements into the home, we sensed that making a connection to nature would give it life. Square footage, equal to more than one of those units, was dedicated just to open space. This gave our client the luxury of taking in the surrounding landscapes from any angle.

"From a long foyer, one enters the home at its most central point and is greeted by spectacular panoramic views of the Hudson River and the rolling hills of New Jersey miles away. By opening and stretching the space, the homeowner is now more connected to the natural elements of their urban environment on a grand scale. Land, sky, the sun's movement, and weather become integral actors in the life of this home."

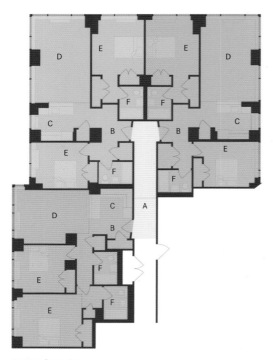

Existing floor plan

A. Building corridor
B. Entry
C. Kitchen
D. Living/dining room
E. Bedroom
F. Bathroom

New floor plan

A. Entry
B. Foyer
C. Living area
D. Laundry room
E. Walk-in closet
F. Office

G. Bathroom
H. Bedroom
I. Dining area
J. Kitchen
K. Breakfast area
L. Sauna

1. Waterfall
2. Fireplace

The open spaces are tied together with a neutral white oak floor that runs through all the rooms, including the bathrooms. The perimeter millwork wraps around the entire home to form windowsills, HVAC covers, storage, and cushioned window seats overlooking the river. The entry hall focuses on the glass waterfall centered in the apartment.

From the center of the living space, panoramic views of downtown, the Hudson River, and the New Jersey hills beyond open up. These views form the backdrop for the dining area. A custom-built stone fireplace marks the space between the dining and living areas.

The master bedroom wing occupies the northwest corner, with an en suite bathroom overlooking the midtown skyline. The guest bedrooms in the south wing share proximity to a custom-built sauna (opposite) situated to take in the sunset over downtown and views of the Statue of Liberty.

Credits

Architect: Andrew Mikhael Architect
www.andrewmikhael.com

Appliances and Materials

Appliances: Miele, Liebherr, and Sub-Zero
Bathroom fixtures: Axor, Duravit, Robern, and Wetstyle
Cabinets and millwork: Poggenpohl
Doors: TRE-Più
Floors: White oak
Furniture and fixtures: B&B Italia, Herman Miller, Modulightor, and Pure Lighting

Kitchen countertop: Silestone
Kitchen faucet: Dornbracht
Kitchen sink: Blanco
Sauna: Saunatec
Walls: Benjamin Moore paint
Water feature: Bluworld

ATTIC CONVERSION

2,583 sq. ft.

Strasbourg, France

---

f+f ARCHITECTS

Photos © Johan Fritzell

Design team: Aurélie Fechter and Johan Fritzell

www.fplusf.fr

> CLEAR OUT THE UPPER FLOOR TO CREATE AN OPEN LIVING AREA

> CREATE A CLEAR DISTINCTION BETWEEN THE ORIGINAL ARCHITECTURAL FEATURES AND THE NEW DESIGN ELEMENTS

THIS LARGE DUPLEX APARTMENT OCCUPIES THE FORMER ATTIC OF AN OLD JUGENDSTIL—OR ART NOUVEAU—BUILDING FROM 1901.

"Originally, it was the space occupied by the maid's rooms and the loft above, which was used for storage. The organization is simple: all rooms— bedrooms, bathrooms, office, family room—are located on the entrance level of the apartment, whereas the top floor is one open loft-like space with kitchen, living, and dining areas. The roof's wood framing provides the space with character. On the other hand, we didn't want it to overpower the space, so we painted it white to blend with the walls and ceiling. This led us to develop a design concept that emphasizes the contrast between old and new.

"The apartment is organized around two major architectural elements: a new staircase under a skylight and a large black box on the lower level. They are both made of Medium-Density Fiberboard dyed in black and stand out within the white-washed shell of the space. By doing so, we achieved a clear distinction between what is preexisting and what is new. Other new elements such as the kitchen cabinetry and the master bathroom's vanity integrate this same material to favor a consistent unity throughout the design."

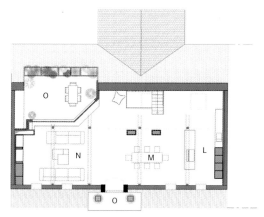

Upper level floor plan

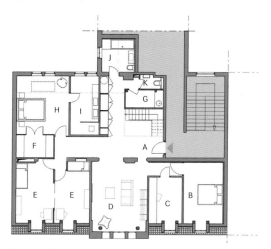

Entry level floor plan

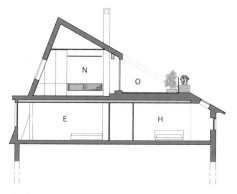

Section

A. Entry hall
B. Guest bedroom
C. Home office
D. Media room
E. Bedroom
F. Walk-in closet
G. Laundry room
H. Master bedroom
I. Master bathroom
J. Bathroom
K. Powder room
L. Kitchen
M. Dining area
N. Living area
O. Terrace

On the upper floor, only the chimney masonry from the apartments on the lower floors interrupts the open plan. The built-in fireplace is flanked with concealed storage and a bar.

The existing varnished pinewood flooring that had become orange-yellow over time was refinished using a Danish lye and soap finish technique to seal the pigmentation and prevent the wood from turning yellow.

In the kitchen, the same Medium-Density Fiberboard has been used for the woodwork and wall paneling. The kitchen island is finished in marble ceramic.

The entry hall is a double height space with a skylight. Its position at the heart of the apartment brings light into the master bedroom, the kids' rooms, guest bedroom, and office space.

The bathroom floor, walls, and countertop are made of large marble ceramic tiles, contrasting with the floating vanity made of black-dyed Medium-Density Fiberboard. The master bedroom is infused with natural light through a new skylight, while an existing small window offers views of a nearby park.

Credits

Architect: f+f Architects
www.fplusf.fr

Appliances and Materials

Aluminum sliding doors: FMS
Appliances: Down draft hood by
Airlux, cooktop by De Dietrich, oven
by Siemens
Bathroom fixtures: Washbasin by
Laufen, faucets and rain shower by
Cristina
Bathroom tiles: Marble ceramic by
Laminam
Fireplace insert: Stüv

Flooring: Woca of Denmark
(Lower floor)
Kitchen island countertop: Marble
ceramic by Laminam
Skylight: Velux
Wallpaper: NLXL (master bedroom)
Wall paneling: Valchromat (staircase
and cabinetry on lower floor; kitchen
on upper floor)

APARTMENT COMBINATION AND TOTAL REMODEL

2,500 sq. ft.

New York, New York, United States

SLAVICA NOVAK NIKOLIC
ARCHITECT / SNNA

Photos © Emily Sidoti Photography and SNNA

Designer: Slavica Novak Nikolic

www.urbanbondcreative.com

> COMBINE A ONE-BEDROOM AND A TWO-
> BEDROOM INTO A LUXURIOUS FOUR-
> BEDROOM APARTMENT

> ENLARGE BATHROOMS

> CREATE A NEW ENTRY AREA THAT
> CORRESPONDS TO THE SIZE AND STYLE OF
> THE NEW APARTMENT

> OPEN THE PLAN FOR THE LOFT-LIKE
> LIVING AND DINING SPACE AND INCLUDE A
> SPACIOUS EAT-IN KITCHEN

> USE THE PRINCIPLES OF FENG SHUI

> USE DIFFERENT CEILING HEIGHTS TO
> ESTABLISH SPATIAL HIERARCHY

SLAVICA NOVAK NIKOLIC CAME HIGHLY RECOMMENDED BY FRIENDS OF THE APARTMENT OWNERS WHO ALSO DID A TWO-APARTMENT COMBINATION USING A TIMELESS AND CLASSIC DESIGN AND INCORPORATING SOME MODERN TOUCHES.

"Two 1960s box apartments with small bathrooms and kitchens and eight-foot ceilings were the starting point. The apartment combination and remodel took into account the clients' desire to have a space where they could entertain. Work included exposing high ceilings wherever possible and using ceiling heights to define hierarchy in the space. It also meant enlarging bathrooms to make them comparable with the rest of the apartment.

"The plan was designed following feng shui principles. An overall sense of harmony and balance was achieved through architectural design itself—elements of space and its relationships—specific use of color, textures, and materials.

"I worked closely with the clients to create a home that is comfortable and pragmatic for family living. The open living and dining area is an inviting entertaining space with built-ins that have met and exceeded storage needs. It also serves as a comfortable place for the family to unwind. With the last piece of furniture in place, the clients have their favorite parts in the apartment: the eat-in kitchen with built-in dining booth and the master bedroom with en suite bathroom. The children love their bedrooms and spacious playroom."

New floor plan

A. Entry foyer   H. Washer/dryer
B. Bathroom   I. Playroom
C. Master bedroom   J. Office
D. Media/Living area   K. Walk-in closet
E. Dining area   L. Master bathroom
F. Kid's bedroom   M. Powder room
G. Eat-in kitchen

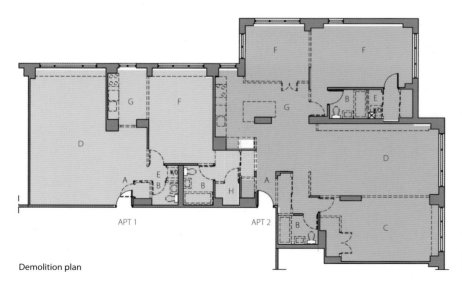

APT 1   APT 2

Demolition plan

A. Entry   E. Washer/dryer
B. Bathroom   F. Bedroom
C. Master bedroom   G. Kitchen
D. Living/dining room H. Closet

Schematic designs

The overall design provides clarity in the organization of the spaces and optimizes the space available.

Wall niches and built-ins animate the rooms and add to their functionality. General lighting and neutral tones are accented with vibrant colors and walnut joinery, creating welcoming and warm spaces.

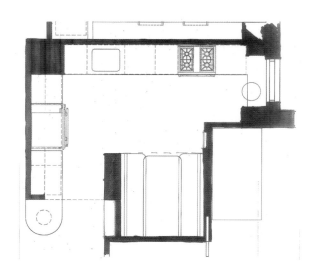

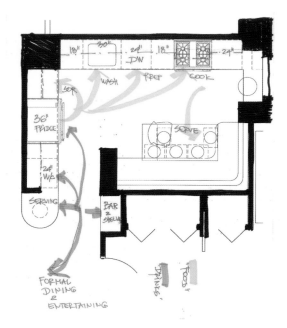

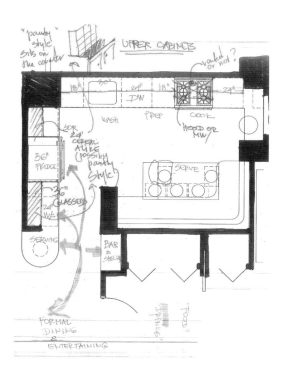

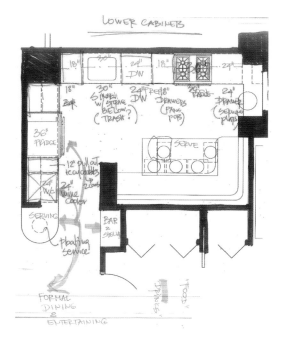

Kitchen's design development plans

By opening up the kitchen to the living area, abundant natural light is let in from the southwest, flooding the apartment with life and luminosity. At the same time, it is conveniently demarcated, yet visually connected to the rest of the spacious living area through a floating counter, built-in bar cabinets, and a wine cooler.

The master bedroom has its own identity with a generous custom designed walk-in closet, enlarged master bathroom, and separate office area.

Slavica invited the kids' input
throughout the design process and
created spaces for them that reflect
their personalities.

Credits

Architect: Slavica Novak Nikolic
Architect / SNNA
www.urbanbondcreative.com

Appliances and Materials

Appliances: Miele, Sub-Zero, and Wolf
Bathroom fixtures: Duravit, Toto, and Hansgrohe
Cabinets: Walnut and painted wood by Neymar and SNNA
Floors: Natural oak, finished on site
Kitchen backsplash: "Fire Brick," Viscaya (glass wall tile) Collection, 4" x 16", clear finish, by Nemo Tile + Stone

Kitchen cabinetry: White melamine cabinets by Downsview
Kitchen countertops: "Blizzard" by Caesarstone
Lighting: Artemide, Flos, Arturo Alvarez, and George Nelson
Walls: Paint and Venetian stucco in foyer

ART COLLECTOR'S LOFT

2,368 sq. ft.

Hong Kong, S.A.R., China

MASS OPERATIONS
Photos © Jonathan Maloney

Designer: Viviano Villarreal-Buerón

www.massoperations.com

> CREATE A SETTING FOR THE DISPLAY OF
  ARTWORK AND BOOK COLLECTION

> MAINTAIN THE OPEN CHARACTER OF
  THE SPACE

> DEVISE A FLOOR PLAN THAT ALLOWS THE
  KITCHEN TO BE PART OF THE LIVING AREA
  OR BE ENCLOSED AS NEEDED

THE OWNER OF THE LOFT IS AN ART COLLECTOR. HIS WISH AS HE AP-
PROACHED OUR DESIGN FIRM WAS TO BE ABLE TO DISPLAY HIS ART
AND BOOK COLLECTION, WHILE ALSO ENTERTAINING GUESTS IN A
COMFORTABLE SETTING WITH VIEWS OF THE CITY.

"The idea of transforming an industrial space into a home was very appealing to us from the very beginning. Industrial spaces are generally a popu-
lar and budget-friendly option for those looking for a unique space. Some
people get very excited about the unusually high ceilings, the generous
open areas, and the interesting design opportunities. There is, of course, the
downside of adapting a space that wasn't originally planned for residential
use into a place with all the living commodities. We were prepared to face
this type of challenge. Turning an industrial space into a livable space often
involves plumbing and ducting work for proper bathrooms and kitchens,
as well as work related to the conservation of fuel and power. Knowing that
and once we had the ball rolling, we were determined to give our client
what he wanted.

"The layout is pragmatic in that it separates the living and sleeping areas.
Opening and closing elements are used to hide and reveal parts of the otherwise completely open space. The kitchen can be opened or closed by
means of large sliding panels that double as blackboards. Our client loved
it! It adds dynamism to the living area. We conceived a similar strategy for
the bedroom. A curtain hides and reveals the closet. It is a simple idea, but it
dramatically changes the character of the space.

"We went for the 'industrial roughness' look: bare concrete beams and columns, and exposed piping and mechanical equipment. We thought that it
would make a great backdrop to our client's art collection. But the result is
that art and architecture complement each other."

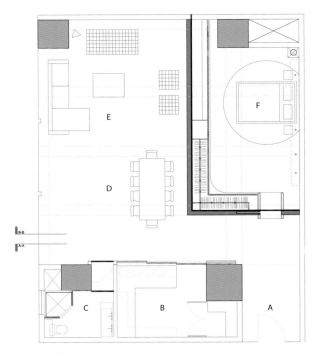

New floor plan

A. Entry hall   D. Dining area
B. Kitchen   E. Living area
C. Bathroom   F. Bedroom

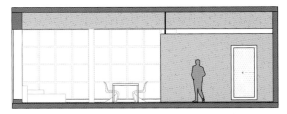

Section B-B

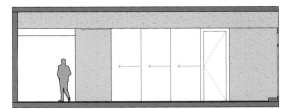

Section A-A

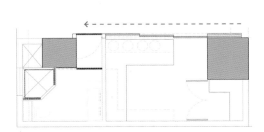

Kitchen detail plan

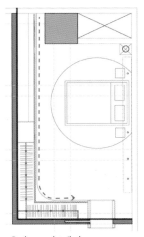

Bedroom detail plan

A new concrete enclosure short
of the ceiling allows for light and
ventilation, while clearly separating
the two realms: public and private.
Because the top of this enclosure
doesn't reach the ceiling, we maintain
a sense of continuity strongly
expressed by the concrete beams.

Floor-to-ceiling blackboard panels add to the industrial look of the space, while at the same time bringing in a clean, slightly reflective surface that contrasts with the roughness of the concrete elements.

Just like the steel panels, the curtain brings in another texture to the material selection. Its soft quality lessens the rough appearance of the loft and contributes to the creation of a more relaxing environment better suited for the bedroom.

Credits

Architect: Mass Operations
www.massoperations.com

General contractor: Hung Limited

Appliances and Materials

Flooring: Epoxy-coated concrete
Walls and ceiling: Painted
plasterboard and exposed concrete
Kitchen panels: Blackboards

LA CASA OF PAUL AND SIGI

2,074 sq. ft.

Montreal, Quebec, Canada

—

MXMA ARCHITECTURE & DESIGN

Photos © Adrien Williams

Design team: Maxime Moreau, architect; Catlin Stothers, Francis Raymond, and Nicolas Labrie

www.mxma.ca

> OPEN UP THE LOWER FLOOR PLAN TO ACCOMMODATE A FLOWING AREA INCLUDING KITCHEN, LIVING, AND DINING AREAS

> USE THE CEILING AS A CONTINUOUS SURFACE THAT GUIDES CIRCULATION THROUGH THE TWO-LEVEL HOME

MXMA ARCHITECTURE & DESIGN WAS INSPIRED BY THE FOLIAGE OF MONTREAL'S LAFONTAINE PARK IN THIS METAMORPHOSIS OF A DUPLEX INTERIOR INTO AN INNOVATIVE LIVING SPACE WITH ABUNDANT WOOD SURFACES.

"This turn-of-the-twentieth-century duplex recently underwent a major interior transformation. As we enter the home at the second-floor level, we discover a vast wooden expanse that gradually unfolds as one looks into the inner reaches of the space. Wood surfaces extend continuously into the space, morphing into floors, walls, ceilings, handrails, and even built-in furniture.

"The organization of the living spaces revolves around the architectural form of the ceiling. The continuity of wood surfaces creates an experience of movement that leads to the third floor, where the more private areas, including three bedrooms and a master suite, are located.

"Technically, it demonstrates how wood can be used to provide flexible and complex solutions with a high-quality finish. Aesthetically, surfaces, materials, and light resonate together to create a living space that emanates warmth.

"There were many structural issues that we had to deal with in order to create an open space with no visible columns or bulkheads. This involved a lot of engineering and steel gymnastics."

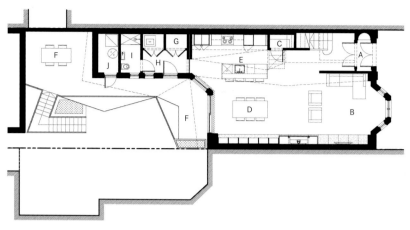

New floor plan

A. Entry   F. Terrace
B. Living area   G. Storage
C. Pantry   H. Vestibule
D. Dining area   I. Bathroom
E. Kitchen   J. Mechanical room

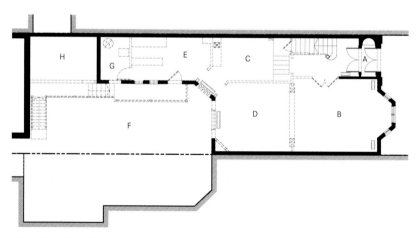

Demolition floor plan

A. Entry   E. Kitchen
B. Living area   F. Interior courtyard
C. Pantry   G. Mechanical room
D. Dining area   H. Storage

Continuity of wooden surfaces becomes the organizing principle of the home's more public areas, such as the entrance, the living room, the dining room, and the kitchen. The irregular surfaces adjust to conceal all the ventilation ducts and the new structure, which includes an imposing steel beam that supports the third floor.

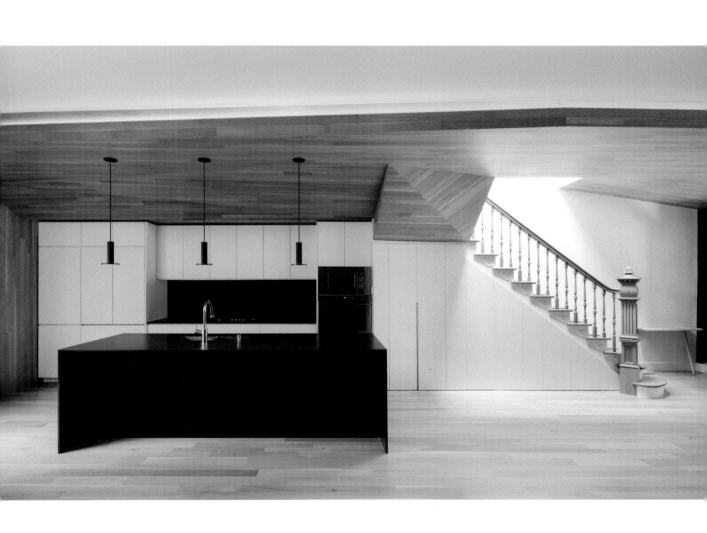

The ceiling adapts to the structure of the existing staircase and then unfolds to become a railing on the third floor. Keeping components of the old front doors, vestibule doors, staircase, railing, spindles, and post, while marrying them with new parts of the same function, was a big challenge.

The woodwork gives the home a sense of expansive continuity as well as a warm and comfortable feel enhanced by natural light.

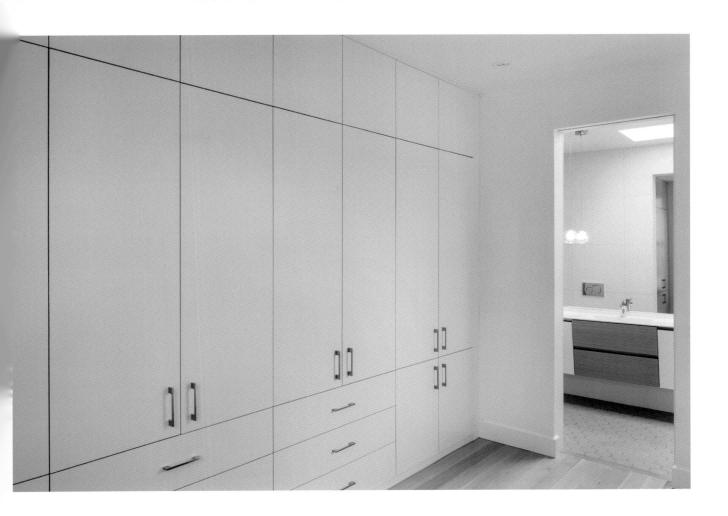

Credits

Architect and interior designer:
MXMA Architecture & Design
www.mxma.ca

General contractor:
Newsam Construction
www.newsam.ca

Structural engineer:
Brian P. Chernoff

Appliances and Materials

Wood: White oak, rift, and quarter-sawn by Bois Franc Lavallée
Kitchen island: Nero assoluto, honed granite by Ardésia, black lacquer, 20% sheen
Kitchen cabinetry: White lacquer, 20% sheen by Unique Cabinet Artisan
Gas fireplace: Valor L1 Linear Series by Nergiflex

Library: Black lacquer, 20% sheen by Dazio
Tiles around fireplace: Laminam Nera Intenso, OTTO Griggio 60 x 120 cm. by Stone Tile
Furniture: Kastella

FIFTH AVENUE RESIDENCE

2,250 sq. ft.

New York, New York, United States

—————

PULLTAB DESIGN
Photos © Mikiko Kikuyama

Design team: Melissa Baker and
Jon Handley

www.pulltabdesign.com

> RELOCATE THE KITCHEN TO A MORE CENTRAL
> AREA

> SEPARATE THE BEDROOMS FROM THE PUBLIC
> AREAS

> LOCATE LIVING ROOM AWAY FROM THE
> DINING ROOM AND KITCHEN TO ALLOW FOR
> MORE FORMAL ENTERTAINING

THE PROJECT IS A COMBINATION OF TWO SMALLER PREWAR APARTMENTS CREATING ONE LARGER RESIDENCE FOR A FAMILY OF FOUR.

"Construction took a year to complete but the result is one of our favorite layouts, where everything lined up right from the beginning. Combining the two apartments presented the opportunity to expand the common areas to favor comfort and flexible use of space. For the couple with two children, we wanted to create common spaces that promote family life and entertaining.

"The original layouts of both apartments didn't really take full advantage of views and exposure. One major change consisted in the relocation of the kitchen to an area that was formerly a bedroom in order to capitalize on the large corner windows. The kitchen is now opened to the dining area. The living area is a bright intimate corner, connected to the rest of the common spaces, yet off to one side, occupying the short wing of the apartment. The private areas take up the opposite end of the renovated combined apartments.

"We had a long hallway to work with, and we made the most of it by lining it with concealed storage. It turned out to be a useful connector between the common and private areas. Circulation was designed to be fluid, so one space would connect with the next seamlessly. We used freestanding built-up walls to frame spaces rather than contain them and to create sight lines that make the home look larger and airier."

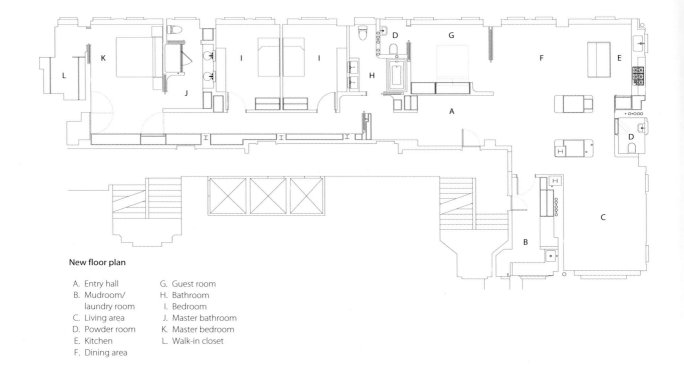

New floor plan

A. Entry hall
B. Mudroom/
   laundry room
C. Living area
D. Powder room
E. Kitchen
F. Dining area
G. Guest room
H. Bathroom
I. Bedroom
J. Master bathroom
K. Master bedroom
L. Walk-in closet

The separation of the bedrooms—the
private zone—from the more public
areas was integral to the design and
works well with the long hallway with
concealed storage, which was used
to join the two original apartments.

Structural columns and building plumbing risers are concealed in new freestanding built-up walls, some of which have millwork cabinetry for storage. This is the case of the two new walls off of the entry hall. One demarcates the kitchen and the other the living room. Together these walls frame a hidden powder room.

Three circular translucent glass windows on the powder room door and the rounded corners of the built-out walls are construction details that contribute to circulation and a fluid connection between different open areas.

The location of the built-up walls allow for sight lines connecting these different areas, while amplifying the perception of the space. Ceiling lights are aligned to accentuate the connection between the formal living room and the kitchen.

While all the living spaces flow into each other, the formal living room feels more contained because the openings connecting it to the kitchen and dining area are narrower. This makes the living area more intimate.

The kitchen island provides a central gathering area—a favorite location for the client's two young boys. The white cabinets blend with the white walls for a homogeneous look. Brass hardware—used throughout the apartment—adds visual interest and picks up on the warm tones of the hardwood floor.

The children's bedrooms have interesting custom built-in furniture that maximizes space, while creating a comfortable nook and adding a playful accent. The designs are sensibly conceived to encourage imagination and creativity.

The master bedroom's millwork highlights a collection of books and artwork, while allowing for clothing storage. A hidden door closes the room from the main hallway.

Poured-in-place terrazzo in the children's bathroom gives a sense of continuity, in line with the concept of the design to create fluid connections between the different areas of the residence, while retro-style mirrors reinforce this effect and echo the curvilinear architectural details.

Credits

Architect: Pulltab Design
www.pulltabdesign.com

Forensic architect: Don Erwin

General contractor: Jim Murray

Structural engineer: Dan Cuoco
and Silman

Appliances and Materials

Floors: 1-1/2"-wide rift oak; poured-in-place terrazzo (children's bathroom and mudroom); custom tile by Heath Ceramics (master bathroom and children's bathroom)
Furniture: Silk carpet from Fort Street Studio, sofa from BDDW, daybed from Ralph Pucci, and other furniture by Christopher Kurtz
Hardware: Custom by Nanz

Lighting: Vintage light fixtures by Helena Tynell and Angelo Lelli; custom light fixtures by Allied Maker, Hervé Van der Straeten, and custom plaster light fixtures by Remains Lighting
Wallpaper: Printed by Marthe Armitage

LAUSANNE

1,905 sq. ft.

São Paulo, Brazil

AR ARQUITETOS
Photos © Maíra Acayaba

Design team: Marina Acayaba and
Juan Pablo Rosenberg

www.ar-arquitetos.com.br

> THE CLIENT WISHED TO HAVE THREE
BEDROOMS, WITH ONE OF THEM AS AN
OFFICE THAT COULD DOUBLE AS A GUEST
ROOM

> ONE OF THE BEDROOMS SHOULD HAVE AN
EN SUITE BATHROOM, WHILE THE OTHER
TWO BEDROOMS WOULD SHARE A COMMON
BATHROOM

> THE KITCHEN SHOULD BE INTEGRATED WITH
THE LIVING ROOM AREA

> THE CLIENTS ALSO WISHED TO MAINTAIN A
SERVICE BATHROOM, AND HAVE A LAUNDRY
AREA THAT ALSO COULD BE USED AS STORAGE

THIS APARTMENT IS LOCATED IN ONE OF THE MOST EMBLEMATIC BUILDINGS OF SÃO PAULO, THE LAUSANNE, DESIGNED BY ARCHITECT FRANZ HEEP IN 1958.

"The client is a young couple from New York with an interest in architecture, art, and design. They wanted the interior to preserve and enhance the building's original features, while at the same time, express a contemporary atmosphere. They provided an extensive list of preferences for the interior design.

"Located on a high floor with multiple windows and north, east, and south exposures, the apartment had very high ceilings and large windows that amplified the space. Great views of the city and a park could be enjoyed from multiple rooms, while a terrace allowed for indoor–outdoor activities.

"Aside from the common difficulties we, as designers, encounter when dealing with remodels, this project presented an unusual challenge. The replacement of windows was under the close scrutiny of a landmark building committee. Our second important challenge involved the relocation of a plumbing stack that went through the middle of our new kitchen layout. Lastly, another challenge was to get our subcontractors to stick to the schedule while the client lived overseas and could not follow the progress closely."

Demolition floor plan

A. Living/dining room
B. Terrace
C. Bedroom
D. Bathroom
E. Kitchen
F. Laundry
G. Maid's room

Demolished
Built

New floor plan

A. Living area
B. Terrace
C. Bedroom
D. Bathroom
E. Kitchen
F. Laundry room
G. Powder room
H. Master bathroom
I. Master bedroom
J. Dining area
K. Lounge

Existing apartment

1

Remodeled apartment

2

Remodeled apartment with metallic shelf

3

Integration of living and dining room and kitchen

4

Metallic shelf

5

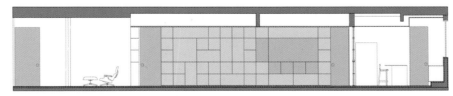

Section

Part of the project consisted of
designing a large metal bookshelf
to delimit the spaces and give the
apartment a contemporary expression
defined by lightness and linearity.

Wood, steel, concrete, and marble are the predominant materials. Exposed concrete surfaces are a reference to Brazilian Brutalist architecture.

The white terrazzo flooring harks back to the 1950s, when the building was constructed and this material was fashionable in São Paulo.

The steel-framed glass partition with doors can either connect or separate the dining area from the kitchen as needed, while allowing natural light from the kitchen's windows to brighten the dining area. The design of the partition also echoes the bookshelf's design.

The kitchen and laundry area were too large for a modern floor plan and had the best light in the entire apartment. The new layout maintains the configuration, while enhancing the design potential of this area.

The client wished to have three bedrooms. One of them serves as both an office and a guest room.

The master bathroom has a refreshing vibe. Its design uses a minimalist approach of colors and materials to enhance details such as the wall-hung basin with its rounded corners, which echoes the shape of the tilt window. The window is an original feature of the apartment building, which was constructed in the late 1950s.

Credits

Architects: Marina Acayaba, Juan Pablo Rosenberg, and Andrea Helou / AR Arquitetos
www.ar-arquitetos.com.br

Interior designer: Marina Acayaba and Juan Pablo Rosenberg / AR Arquitetos and Cassiana Basso, apartment owner / otherstudio
www.otherstudio.com

Lighting designer: Rafael Leão
www.rafaelleao.com

Appliances and Materials

Floors: Terrazzo and existing parquet floor
Walls: Paint
Kitchen: Adresse
Countertop and backsplash: "Absolute Black" granite
Sink and faucet: Roca and Newport Brass
Appliances: Liebherr, Tecno, and Tecnogas

Cabinets: White lacquered MDF
Furniture and fixtures: Cassina, Cappellini, L'Atelier, Jader Almeida, Sergio Rodrigues, Oscar Niemeyer, Flos, and Omega Light

FLATIRON LOFT MEETS BALI

1,900 sq. ft.

New York, New York, United States

MATIZ ARCHITECTURE AND DESIGN
Photos © StudioAbe

Design team: Juan Carlos Matiz AIA, Sara Matiz, Marlene Mendez, and Sloan Springer

www.mad-nyc.com

> BRING THE BALI EXPERIENCE INTO THE RENOVATION DESIGN

> GIVE THE SPACES FOR SHARED FAMILY ACTIVITIES AND THE MASTER BEDROOM PROPER DESIGN ATTENTION

> UPGRADE THE KITCHEN AND THE TWO BATHROOMS

THE DESIGN FOR THIS MIDTOWN MANHATTAN LOFT WAS INFLUENCED BY THE OWNERS' LOVE FOR BALI, WHERE THE FAMILY HAD VACATIONED JUST MONTHS PRIOR TO BEGINNING THE RENOVATION OF THEIR HOME.

"The building's prior life as a manufacturing facility provided expansive ceiling heights and large windows that permitted quality natural light to enter the residential unit. This family of five was looking to carefully upgrade the apartment and bring some of their Bali experience into the material palette of the apartment.

"The entry was particularly awkward. This triggered the beginning of the redesign work. After reorienting the front door and properly addressing the living room's furniture layout, we developed schemes for the way the kitchen and dining areas would coexist. The kitchen had to be open to the living room. We also had to integrate the client's art collection. This was resolved by constucting a colorful wall of metal containers brought from Bali, making a strong design statement, while working together with the owner's art collection.

"Creating a den was also a goal. This central space became the mixing bowl to which the various bedrooms and second bath would reference. Once the various parts were outlined, the materials, lighting, and furnishing took center stage. These new elements work together with the rawness of the exposed structural beams, sprinkler lines, and ductwork, which reference the history of the building prior to its current residential use."

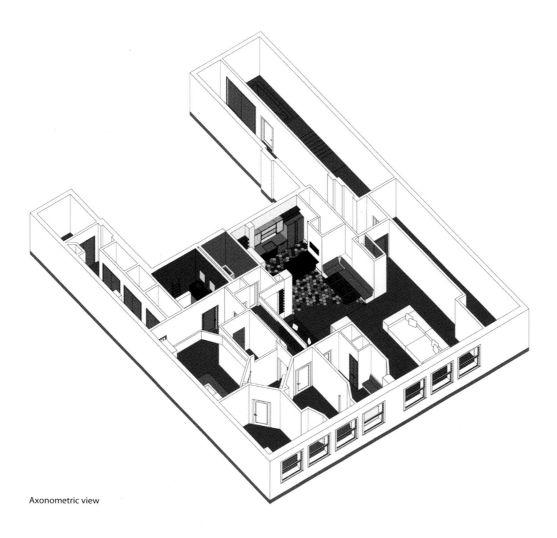

Axonometric view

At the planning stage, it was evident that some aspects of the loft worked fairly well, such as the number and size of the bedrooms located along the street-facing façade. The master bedroom was contrived and needed proper definition, while the two bathrooms, kitchen, and the spaces for shared family activities needed serious upgrading.

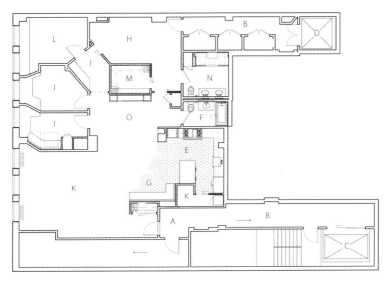

New floor plan

A. Entry
B. Building corridor
C. Passenger elevator
D. Freight elevator
E. Kitchen
F. Bathroom
G. Dining area
H. Dressing area

I. Bedroom
J. Study
K. Living area
L. Master bedroom
M. Walk-in closet
N. Master bathroom
O. Den

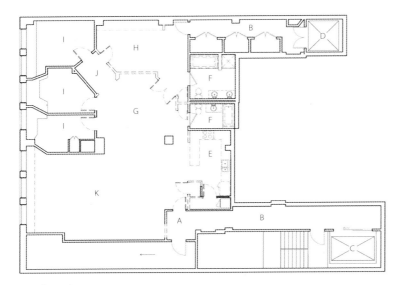

Demolition plan

A. Entry
B. Building corridor
C. Passenger elevator
D. Freight elevator
E. Kitchen
F. Bathroom

G. Dining area
H. Dressing area
I. Bedroom
J. Study
K. Living area

A cozy informal den sits just outside the four bedrooms and offers the family a more casual space for TV watching and entertainment. A custom millwork unit acts as the focal point for this area.

Immediately next to the den is
the kitchen, which is formed by a
combination of gray off-the-shelf
cabinets and custom panels.
This design gives the kitchen a
unique feel, contrasted by the New
York subway tile wall and backsplash.

The children's bathroom has a bright blue mosaic tile wall with their names inscribed in white, affording a truly customized design that is both playful and timeless. In contrast, the master bathroom has subdued tones. It uses petrified wood for a custom bench in the two-person shower, while another piece is used at the custom-designed vanity. Needless to say, the petrified wood was brought from Bali.

Credits

Architect:
Matiz Architecture and Design
www.mad-nyc.com

General contractor:
Unlimited Renovation

Appliances and Materials

Appliances: BI-42S 42" built-in, side-by-side fridge by Sub-Zero; "Pureline" 60 cm microwave oven by Miele; DF484CG 48" dual fuel range by Wolf; and PL342212 34-3/8" Pro Ventilation Hood Liner by Wolf
Doors: Reclaimed NYC public school doors
Fixtures: "Atrio" three-hole basin mixer (bathroom); "Handle Jota" sink

(kids' bathroom); "Cosmopolitan 210" showerhead and 16" shower arm (bathroom); wall-hung toilet by Lacava (bathroom)
Floors: Stained white oak by Rubio Monocoat and 20 x 20 cm hexagon, "Urban Tile" by Pesamuan Ceramic (kitchen)
Kitchen cabinets: By IKEA

Walls: SCIS, "Waterglass Bluedstreak" and "Natural Snow" by Benjamin Moore (kids' bathroom); 12" x 24" Durastone "Steel Gray" stream porcelain and 12" x 24" "Lavacode Honed" by Cancos Tile (master bathroom)

EAST 90TH STREET APARTMENT

1,800 sq. ft.

New York, New York, United States

S4ARCHITECTURE
Photos © Beatrice Pediconi

Design team: Michele Busiri-Vici and Clementina Ruggieri, architects; Annie Mennes, project manager

www.space4architecture.com

> TRANSFORM A SPACE ORIGINALLY OVER-
COMPARTMENTALIZED INTO AN OPEN FLOOR
PLAN

SPACIOUS AND BRIGHT APARTMENT WITH STAGGERING VIEWS OVER MADISON AVENUE

"The apartment has reasonably high ceilings. It was all about opening up the space and keeping partitions to a minimum. We successfully created a public zone that is very open, while the private zone is more intimate.

"Keeping the wall along Madison Avenue uninterrupted was definitely key in order to make the public zone as open as possible. Also, using see-through built-in units and floor-to-ceiling sliding panels contributed to this effect. The result was a continuous and light-filled space shared by the kitchen, living, and dining areas.

"In contrast, the private zones have more intimate proportions and more contained, cozy spaces.

"As for the materials, we wanted to keep most finishes neutral so we used colors that don't overpower the spaces and that you don't get tired of easily. This actually gave the clients more freedom with their selection of furniture."

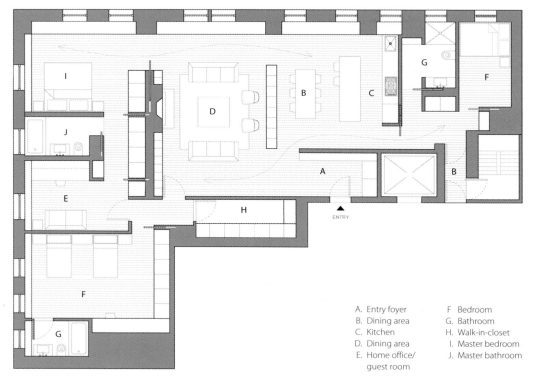

New floor plan

A. Entry foyer
B. Dining area
C. Kitchen
D. Dining area
E. Home office/
   guest room

F Bedroom
G. Bathroom
H. Walk-in-closet
I. Master bedroom
J. Master bathroom

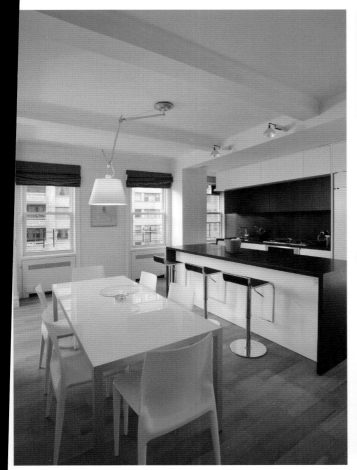

The kitchen features "Black Absolut" finished island and custom white lacquer cabinets.

The master and children's bathrooms
have poured-in-place concrete floors,
glass tiles, and custom millwork.

Credits

Architect: S4Architecture
www.space4architecture.com

General contractor: Diagrama

Appliances and Materials

Appliances: Gaggenau
Carpentry: Custom millwork
Floors: White oak with custom stain, poured-in-place concrete
Ligthing: Deltalight, Flos, Artemide, and AAMSCO
Plumbing fixtures: Duravit, Dornbracht, and Laufen

Walls: Level 5 skim coat, painted white; custom-colored plaster and glass tiles (bathrooms only)

ARCHITECTURE IN FORMATION

Photos © Michelle Rose and
Architecture in Formation

Design team: **Matthew Bremer AIA,** Principal-in-charge, **Paulo Flores**, project manager, **Ryan Barnett**, job captain

www.aifny.com

> COMBINE TWO APARTMENTS INTO A
COMFORTABLE TWO-BEDROOM HOME

> CREATE A GOURMET KITCHEN OPEN TO THE
LIVING AND DINING AREAS

THIS APARTMENT'S OWNER SEIZED AN OPPORTUNITY TO EXPAND HIS BACHELOR PAD INTO A LARGER HOME WHEN AN ADJACENT STUDIO WAS PUT UP FOR SALE AND HE BECAME ENGAGED.

"A young bachelor had acquired a two-bedroom, two-bath apartment in a mid-century building on one of Greenwich Village's most sought-after streets. He had his parents' architect do some simple renovations, including a small kitchen and a bathroom.

"About two years later, the adjacent studio apartment became available just as he became engaged. Properly combining the two apartments was a sizable task that involved a reconfiguration of the two apartments, including the portion he had just completed two years earlier.

"The studio, located in the quiet rear of the building, allowed for a comfortable and private master bedroom suite. In turn, this allowed for the opportunity to open up the entire front of the apartment, converting the existing bedroom into a full dining room. The second bedroom, which served as study and guest room, was converted into a nursery as they prepared to start their family.

"The couple's love for entertaining, and particularly his interest in cooking, required a kitchen suitable to such tasks and pleasures. Its design followed a sculptural approach. Crisp white plaster walls and wide white oak plank floors formed the backdrop for a dramatic kitchen of pearwood and gray Corian.

"The project resulted in a large—by Manhattan standards—two-bedroom apartment, which can be expanded into a three-bedroom, if necessary. The clients love their home, which they share with their dog Dakota."

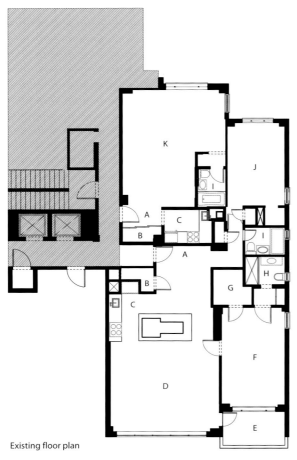

Existing floor plan

A. Entry hall   G. Walk-in closet
B. Closet   H. Master bathroom
C. Kitchen   I. Bathroom
D. Living/dining area   J. Bedroom
E. Balcony   K. Studio
F. Master bedroom

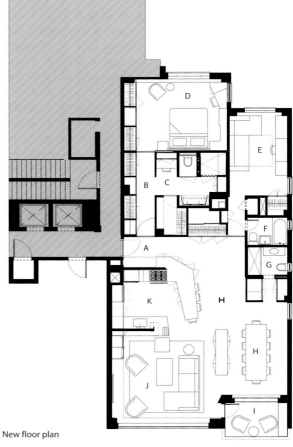

New floor plan

A. Entry hall   G. Bathroom
B. Master closet   H. Dining area
C. Master bathroom   I. Balcony
D. Master bedroom   J. Living area
E. Guest bedroom   K. Kitchen
F. Guest bathroom

The spacious, dramatic kitchen is the focal point for the couple's frequent entertaining. Different ceiling heights and dramatic lighting combine to distinguish the different areas that comprise the open plan, avoiding the need for partitioning.

Custom pear wood veneer cabinet
fronts and paneling, Corian countertops,
and clever details such as the integrated
dog-feeding tray designed by the
architect make the kitchen the
centerpiece of the living area.

The dining table occupies a luminous corner of the spacious great room with windows on two sides.

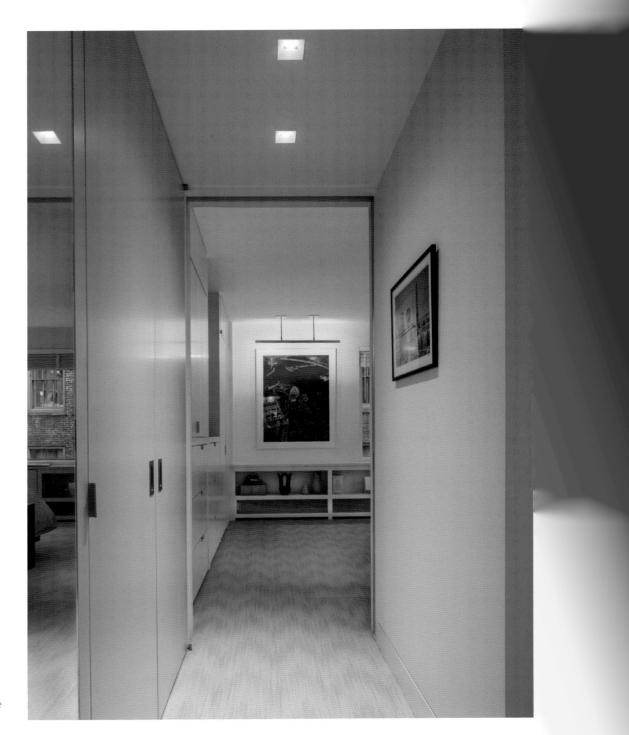

The master closet serves as buffer between the social spaces and the master bedroom.

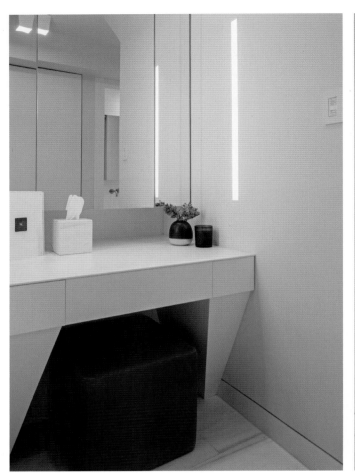

The new design gives the small
bathroom off of the living area and
the master bathroom big appeal
with an all-white color scheme that
amplifies the perception of the space.

Credits

Architect: Architecture in Formation
www.aifny.com

General contractor: All City
Remodeling

Appliances and Materials

Bathroom fixtures: Vola
Floors: Rift cut white oak plank
Kitchen: Custom pear wood veneer
cabinetry with Corian counters
Master bathroom stone: Stone Source

MARINE LOFT

1,750 sq. ft.

Santa Monica, California, United States

SUBU DESIGN ARCHITECTURE

Photos © Manolo Langis

Design team: **May Sung,** AIA, Design principal
and **Jim Burkholder,** Principal/project manager

www.subuda.com

> CREATE A DESIGN WITH NATURAL ELEMENTS

> RESPECT THE ORIGINAL INDUSTRIAL
CHARACTER OF THE APARTMENT

SUBU TRANSFORMED THIS INDUSTRIAL SPACE CLOSE TO THE BEACH INTO A HOME INCORPORATING NATURAL ELEMENTS. THE OWNER'S PASSION FOR NATURE AND SURFING WAS THE STARTING POINT FOR THE REDESIGN.

"The loft is located on the third floor of a commercial building located one block from the beach. Architecturally, the existing interior was a white box with industrial components.

"The client is a Korean American banker, raised in the Midwest, and relocating from New York City. An avid surfer who embraces the California lifestyle, he wanted a home with natural elements, while respecting the industrial character of the space.

"We wanted to create different areas while avoiding physical separations. From the entry, the loft reveals itself as a long space with a central island made out of reclaimed logs. The lengthy island emphasizes the horizontality of the space, while directing the eye toward the far end, occupied by the living and dining areas. The linearity of the space is further emphasized by a retractable garage door, which, when opened, exposes the interior to the outdoors.

"Finding the right construction materials was perhaps the biggest challenge. Looking for the right reclaimed wood for the construction of the kitchen island and the bed platform was not easy, but eventually we were able to find a source on the East Coast that had exactly the wood with the age patina we were looking for. We then had to transport the huge pieces of wood across the country for assembly on site. I worked closely with the contractor to find the best construction method and detailing with the best results."

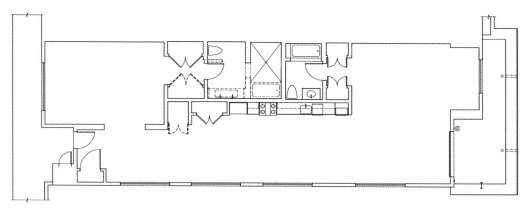

Existing floor plan

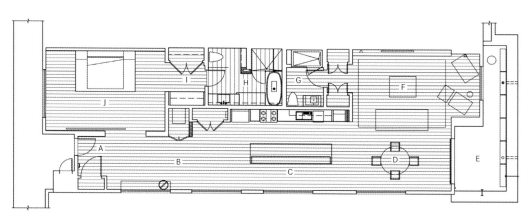

New floor plan

A. Entry
B. Wine and cigar area
C. Kitchen
D. Dining area
E. Balcony
F. Living area
G. Bathroom
H. Master bathroom
I. Walk-in closet
J. Bedroom

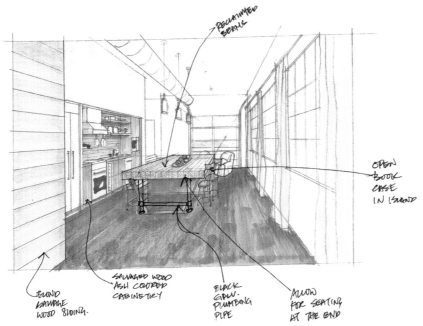

RECLAIMED
BEAMS

OPEN
BOOK
CASE
IN ISLAND

SALVAGED WOOD
ASH COLORED
CABINETRY

SECOND
SALVAGE
WOOD SIDING.

BLACK
GALV.
PLUMBING
PIPE

ALLOW
FOR SEATING
AT THE END

Design development study

The design of the loft was thoughtfully developed to integrate a selection of natural and industrial materials.

The back of the apartment has a sectional garage door with transparent panels. It slides up and then back along the ceiling to open up completely the apartment to the outside.

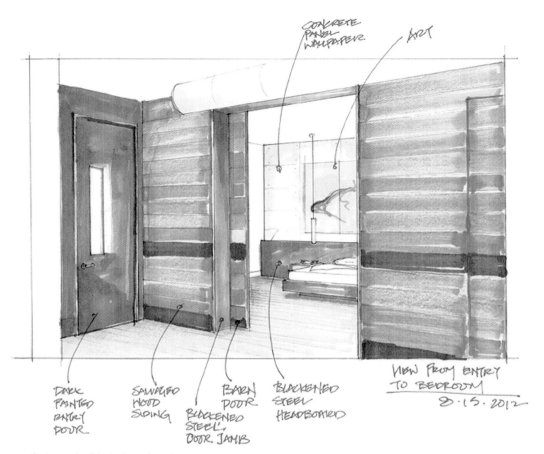

CONCRETE
PANEL
WALLPAPER

ART

DARK
PAINTED
ENTRY
DOOR

SALVAGED
WOOD
SIDING

BARN
DOOR

BLACKENED
STEEL,
DOOR JAMB

BLACKENED
STEEL
HEADBOARD

VIEW FROM ENTRY
TO BEDROOM
8·15·2012

Design study of the bedroom barn doors

For the bedroom, we created a large sleeping platform with bent blackened steel panels to serve as bedside tables.

The bathroom's design explores the nautical theme to its maximum with salvaged wood siding reminiscent of driftwood, a porthole mirror, and a nautical pendant above a stone sink.

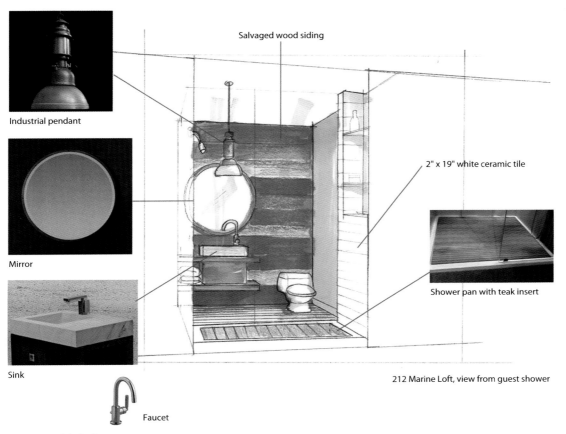

Industrial pendant

Mirror

Sink

Faucet

Design study of the bathroom

Salvaged wood siding

2" x 19" white ceramic tile

Shower pan with teak insert

212 Marine Loft, view from guest shower

Credits

Architect and interior designer:
SUBU Design Architecture
www.subuda.com

General contractor:
Tommy Van Lokeren

Appliances and Materials

Appliances: GE Monogram
Countertop and backsplash: Stone
from Walker Zanger
Floors: Antique French oak
Sink and faucet: From Waterworks
Walls: reclaimed wood and paint

**SLAVICA NOVAK NIKOLIC
ARCHITECT / SNNA**
Photos © Image Works NYC and SNNA

Designer: Slavica Novak Nikolic

www.urbanbondcreative.com

> COMBINE TWO NEIGHBORING APARTMENTS

> RECONFIGURE ENTRY HALL

> CREATE A SPACIOUS LIVING AREA THAT
  REFLECTS THE GRAND NATURE OF THE
  BUILDING

THE DESIGN, WHICH COMBINES TWO ADJACENT APARTMENTS INTO ONE,
LIVES UP TO THE HIGH STANDARDS OF THE BUILDING THEY BELONG TO.

"The project combines two neighboring apartments on the twenty-third floor of a recently built Michael Graves luxury condo building on the Upper East Side. The client wished to create a comparable lavish space in the spirit of the building. The entry lobby was redesigned with decorative niches and flooring detail to give a formal and elegant feeling to the apartment.

"The main area is stately and sophisticated, with lighting as one of the most important design elements. Lighting, both natural and artificial, works on two levels: first, it brightens up the entire place and second, it accentuates specific areas and architectural features. Juxtaposed with the lighting opulence is an almost frugal color palette—whites and natural wood—which allows for a rich play of shadows. Lighting is also an integral part of the design of key elements such as the kitchen island, enhancing form and materiality. Overall, the materials are simple yet effective choices. They contribute to the creation of the desired elegant décor and relaxed atmosphere."

A. Entry
B. Bathroom
C. Bedroom
D. Dining area
E. Kitchen
F. Master bedroom
G. Master bathroom
H. Walk-in closet
I. Living area

New floor plan with adjoining foyer

A. Entry
B. Bathroom
C. Bedroom
D. Living/dining room
E. Kitchen
F. Master bathroom
G. Master bedroom

Existing floor plan

The original layouts of the apartments consisted of small enclosed kitchens and tight living–dining areas. This constrained feeling was minimized with a new layout that combines three bays into one large living and dining area with windows on two sides.

A grand entry hall was devised to reflect the character of the building and give a taste of the spaciousness. The newly created foyer with decorative niche and flooring medallion detail gives a formal luxurious feeling to the apartment.

The kitchen consists of two areas: a functional wall lined with maple wood cabinets and stainless steel appliances and a sculptural island, which constitutes the social part of the kitchen, more integrated into the living and dining area.

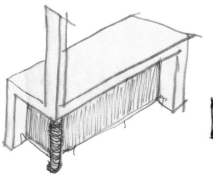

Sketches of kitchen island

Dropped ceilings, punctuated
with different types of lights, help
differentiate the spaces. Lighting is
an integral part of the island design,
reinforcing its form and turning it into
a focal point in the open area.

The bathroom is simple, clean, and elegant. The statuary white marble and dark-stained cherry vanity on one side and a storage bench of the same materials on the other accentuate the horizontality of the room. This is further emphasized by the storage bench turning into a shower seat opposite the glass.

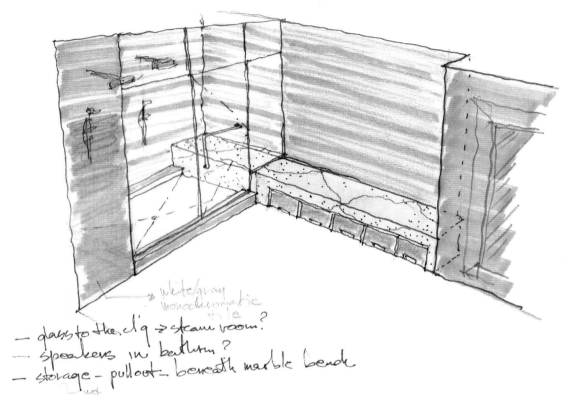

→ white/gray
monochromatic
tile

— glass to the clg → steam room?
— speakers in bathrm?
— storage - pullout - beneath marble bench

Sketch of master bathroom

Credits

**Architect: Slavica Novak Nikolic
Architect / SNNA**
www.urbanbondcreative.com

Appliances and Materials

Appliances: Miele, Sub-Zero, and Viking
Bathroom fixtures: Kohler, Toto, Hansgrohe
Cabinets: Neymar and SNNA
Floors: Oak floor with custom made medallion
Kitchen backsplash: "Baton Pavarotti Pearl", mix of gloss and satin stilato mosaic, Opera Glass Collection, by Artistic Tile

Kitchen cabinetry: Maple cabinets by Kraftmade
Kitchen countertops: "Yucon Blanco" by Silestone on countertop, island, and stone cladding
Lighting: Artemide and Flos
Walls: Paint and Venitian stucco in foyer

1,600 sq. ft.

New York, New York, United States

—

BILLINKOFF ARCHITECTURE

Photos © Jon DeCola

Designer: Donald Billinkoff

www.billinkoff.com

> CONNECT INTERIOR SPACE AND TERRACE

> ACCOMMODATE ART COLLECTION

> OPEN UP KITCHEN TO DINING AND
   LIVING AREAS

> OPTIMIZE STORAGE SPACE THROUGHOUT THE
   APARTMENT

DOWNSIZING FROM A 7,000-SQ.-FT. FAMILY HOME IN WESTCHESTER TO A TWO-BEDROOM POST-WAR MANHATTAN APARTMENT DEMANDS A VAST NUMBER OF PRACTICAL DECISIONS WITH CONSIDERABLE EMOTIONAL IMPACT. OUR CLIENTS EMBARKED ON THIS TRANSITION WITH SOME TREPIDATION.

"The apartment our clients purchased offered no hint of any potential. It was located in a ubiquitous Upper East Side 1960s white brick building; one of those buildings characterized by eight-foot ceilings, aluminum windows, poor quality finishes, and a dearth of sunlight. However, it did have one thing going for it: an outdoor terrace the new owners were allowed to enclose and thereby annex to the living space.

"Our clients requested the apartment have a contemporary urban feel and be suitable for large family gatherings. Thoughtful storage solutions were a must. All existing furniture was negotiable. If a piece worked, it would come, and if not, it would be sent to storage, given away, or sold. The only thing that had to be accommodated was the art collection they had assembled over many years. To achieve a light, bright floor that could serve as a background to the art, we chose a 24-inch-square terrazzo tile. It was used throughout the apartment, except in the den and master bedroom, where floors were carpeted. Two wood finishes were combined: a rich walnut to add warmth and a light finish TABU veneer. Accents are blackened steel and charcoal-colored quartz.

"The renovation took six months to complete and resulted in a dramatic change. Aside from the windows, it is difficult to recognize the apartment's origin. It reflects our clients' passion for art and recasts their home as warm and contemporary, which is exactly what they wanted."

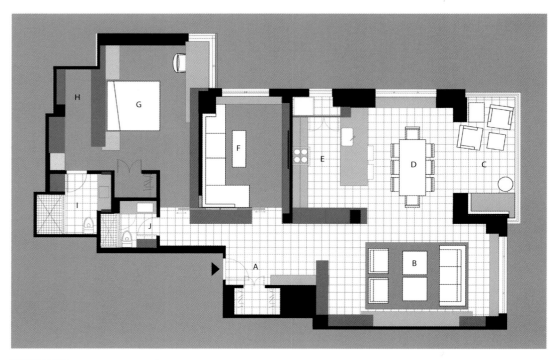

New floor plan

A. Entry hall
B. Living area
C. Lounge
D. Dining area
E. Kitchen
F. Media room
G. Master bedroom
H. Walk-in closet
I. Master bathroom
J. Bathroom

Custom millwork demarcates the apartment's different areas without sacrificing openness and fluid circulation. Structural beams and columns are encased within the millwork, leaving no trace of the original layout.

To showcase the owners' art as well as to provide storage, we designed millwork to wrap around the living room. At a height of 42 inches, it accommodates sculpture on its long top shelf and in steel-lined niches below. To accommodate overflow seating, an upholstered leather bench was integrated into the cabinetry.

The wall separating the kitchen
and dining room was removed and
replaced with an oversized serving
counter. Millwork at one end of
the kitchen screens a utility closet
accommodating a washer and dryer.

The outdoor terrace and the interior space were connected. The original sliding glass doors that originally separated the two areas were removed, the ceiling and floor heights aligned, and the exterior brick was covered with Sheetrock to create a sense of continuity. Floor-to-ceiling glass was used to to enhance the lofty atmosphere.

To optimize storage, compartments
in the master bedroom were
completely built in. A closet separates
the dressing area from the bedroom.
Its bedroom side is upholstered
to work as a headboard. Opposite
this stands a full wall of cabinetry
incorporating desk, filing cabinets,
bookshelves, TV, and a large wooden
sculpture that formerly hung in the
owners' living room.

Credits

Architect: Billinkoff Architecture
www.billinkoff.com

Cabinetry:
Jorge Oliveira/Art Woodworking

General contractor:
Ron Bo/KRS Renovation

Appliances and Materials

Entry hall bench and lounge chair:
Donald Billinkoff
Floors: "Perla Blanca," #616, 24" x 24",
by Daltile
Kitchen counters: "Armani Grey," polis-
hed, 3/4" thick slab, by Quartz Master
Living and dining room furniture:
owner

Master bathroom: Marvel (Porcelain)
Collection, "Calacatta Extra," polished,
12" x 24", by Nemo Tile & Stone
Master bedroom bed and side tables:
Donald Billinkoff
Powder room: Marvel (Porcelain)
Collection, "Grey Stone," polished,
12" x 24", by Nemo Tile & Stone

BEATTY STREET LOFT

1,500 sq. ft.*

Vancouver, British Columbia, Canada

———

FALKEN REYNOLDS INTERIORS

Photos © Ema Peter Photography

*1,100 living space + 400-sq.-ft. covered patio

Design team: Chad Falkenberg and Kelly
Reynolds, principals

www.falkenreynolds.com

> CREATE OPEN SPACES SUITABLE FOR BOTH
WORKING FROM HOME AND HOSTING LARGE
GATHERINGS

> ORIENT THE KITCHEN TO HAVE BETTER VIEWS
OF THE TV, AND CREATE FLEXIBLE SPACES
TO PULL IN STOOLS AND CHAIRS FOR EXTRA
SEATING AROUND THE TV

A BROOKLYN WAREHOUSE—INSPIRED LOFT FOR A PROFESSIONAL COUPLE LIVING BETWEEN NEW YORK AND VANCOUVER RECEIVES AN EXTENSIVE MAKEOVER.

"The clients are huge sports fans and so there is always a game on TV. By orienting the kitchen towards the sitting room, the clients can prepare meals and host large gatherings without missing the game.

"We created a dining room from a storage room and shower, added comfortable seating at the kitchen island, and a dining table on the covered patio. These were the key elements that guided the design. Once we had these elements defined, everything fell into place, including finishes, colors, additional furnishings, light fixtures, and accessories.

"A modern take on Craftsman elements combined with the richness of oiled walnut and hints of black give the space a distinctly elegant feel, referencing the clients' bi-coastal cosmopolitan lifestyles."

A 400-square-foot outdoor living and dining patio is an extension of the living and dining area. A seamless connection is partly achieved by extending interior materials to the exterior.

Emphasizing the 19-foot ceilings is a Bocci chandelier composed of 18 glass spheres cascading over the island. The herringbone glass backsplash reflects light from the exterior.

New lower floor plan

A. Entry	F. Terrace	1. Fireplace
B. Powder room	G. Walk-in closet	2. BBQ
C. Dining area	H. Master bathroom	3. Fridge
D. Kitchen	I. Bedroom	4. Washer and dryer
E. Living area		5. Open to below

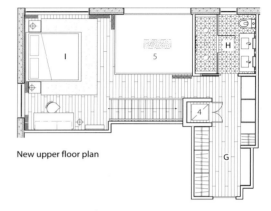

New upper floor plan

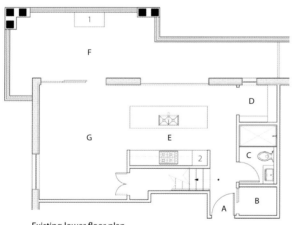

Existing lower floor plan

A. Entry	F. Patio	1. Fireplace
B. Storage	G. Living area	2. Fridge
C. Bathroom	H. Dressing room	3. Washer and dryer
D. Nook	I. Master bathroom	4. Open to below
E. Kitchen	J. Bedroom	

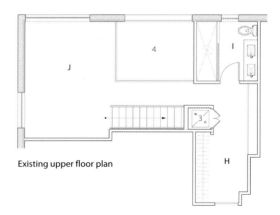

Existing upper floor plan

Metal Vitsœ shelving, thin stone countertops, natural linen drapery, and pieces of furniture that balance heavy forms with slim legs emphasize the openness of the apartment.

The shape of the en suite vanity gives a lightweight effect in line with the general concept of the apartment's design. The rhomboid floor tiles and wood vanity add pattern and texture to contrast the flat finishes of the subway tile and paint.

Credits

Architect and interior designer:
Falken Reynolds Interiors
www.falkenreynolds.com

Appliances and Materials

Appliances: Concealed fridge and dishwasher, gas cooktop, convection oven, food fan, and wine cooler by Miele
Dining area lighting: Brass Lindvall pendant by Wästberg through Inform Interiors
En suite countertop: "Clamshell" 4130, polished finish by Caesarstone
Floors: Tex Series porcelain tile, black color, by Mutina through Stone Tile; European white oak, Sahara oiled, Mozart collection by European Touch Hardwood
Kitchen countertop: "Bianco Drift" 6131, polished finish by Caesarstone
Kitchen lighting: Pendant chandelier Bocci 28.16 by Bocci through Inform Interiors; String Lights by Flos through Inform Interiors

Walls: "Arctic White" subway tile, matte finish, Colour & Dimension Series, through Olympia Tile+Stone; herringbone pattern, "Aqua Beryl", Glasstints Series by Interstyle; OC-55 "Paper White" by Benjamin Moore, "Cucumber" SW 6722 by Sherwin Williams, "Cityscape" SW 7067 by Sherwin Williams

WEST 67TH STREET RESIDENCE

1,350 sq. ft.

New York, New York, United States

ALEXANDER BUTLER | DESIGN SERVICES

Photos © Elk Studios

Designer: Alexander Butler

www.abdsnyc.com

> RENOVATE, KEEPING IN MIND FUTURE
RESALE

> OPEN UP KITCHEN TO LIVING AREA

> RENOVATE BATHROOMS AND BEDROOMS
WITH NEW FINISHES, FIXTURES, AND
FURNITURE

> ADD STORAGE SPACE

> USE INNOVATIVE PRODUCTS AND MATERIALS
TO ACHIEVE A HIGH-END LOOK, WHILE
MAINTAINING A SENSITIVITY TO A BUDGET

THE FACELIFT OF AN OUTDATED APARTMENT FOCUSED ON THE CRE-ATION OF A MORE FUNCTIONAL PLAN WITH ADDED STORAGE SPACE AND UPGRADED FINISHES.

"In addition to being particularly interesting to me because this project was my first fully realized built work, it was a very illuminating study in materials. My in-laws own the apartment and my wife had lived there for ten years before meeting me. After we got married and I moved in, they asked me to undertake the renovation, keeping in mind the future resale of the unit.

"Taking down the galley kitchen wall to open up the space was fundamental to the transformation and to achieve the ultimate loft living experience. Removing the window seat storage in the living area uncovered two feet of glazing. That storage was replaced with taller and more useful storage in the interior of the apartment.

"We didn't want to sacrifice the design, so we did some intensive material research, which gave rise to some very successful results. All of the bathrooms and bedrooms received a facelift. The master bedroom entry was once at one end of a ten-foot hallway. Once it was relocated, it was possible to occupy that space, combined with the existing bedroom closets, to create one large L-shaped space, tripling the square footage of the new closet.

"Caesarstone was without question an economical alternative to natural stone, as were wood-grain-look porcelain floors relative to wide-plank wood flooring. An innovative new Formica laminate product was added to the list of materials that slashed the millwork budget by several magnitudes.

"Many clients and designers would otherwise disparage these materials, but I've learned that they are incredibly successful alternatives to typical high-end luxury items, and I present these possibilities to everyone I work with."

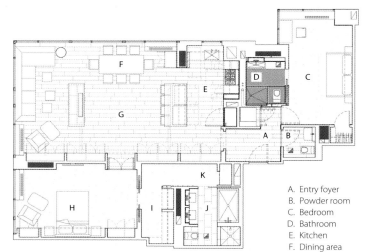

New floor plan

A. Entry foyer
B. Powder room
C. Bedroom
D. Bathroom
E. Kitchen
F. Dining area
G. Living area
H. Master bedroom
I. Master closet
J. Master bathroom
K. Hall

Existing floor plan

A. Entry foyer
B. Powder room
C. Bedroom
D. Bathroom
E. Kitchen
F. Living/dining area
G. Master bedroom
H. Master bathroom

1. Remove electric radiator, but retain power
2. Remove base around column
3. Remove window seats
4. Remove AC covers
5. Remove all wood flooring and substrate
6. Demolish to the extent possible
7. Remove carpet, but retain and protect wood flooring
8. Remove window sill
9. Remove doors
10. Remove all appliances
11. Remove all flooring, countertops, and cabinetry
12. Remove all tile flooring
13. Existing FPSC fire door to remain
14. Remove sinks, toilet, and bathtub
15. Remove all fixtures and fittings
16. Remove all flooring and vanity
17. Remove sink, toilet, all fixtures, and fittings
18. Remove sink, toilet, all fixtures, fittings, and flooring
19. Retain closet interiors

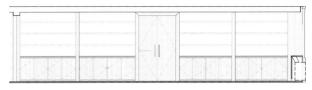

Living room north elevation

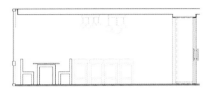

Living room west elevations

Living room east elevation

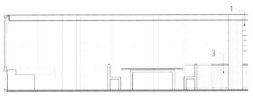

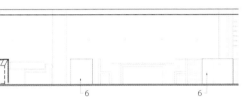

Living room south elevations

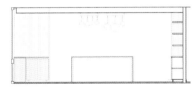

Kitchen west elevations

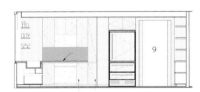

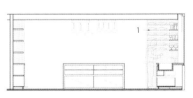

Kitchen east elevation

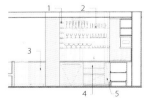

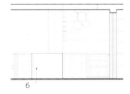

Kitchen south elevations

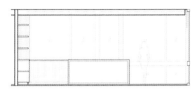

1. Wood wine rack
2. Glass shelves
3. Movable bar cart
4. False drawer
5. Step ladder drawer
6. Custom Caesarstone kitchen island
7. Drawers behind
8. Pull-out pantry
9. Open to foyer

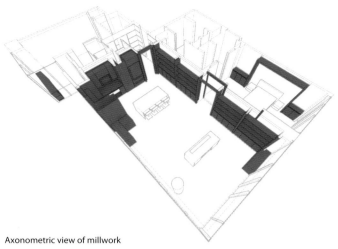

Axonometric view of millwork

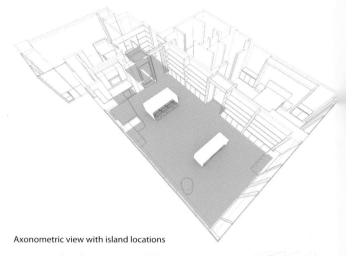

Axonometric view with island locations

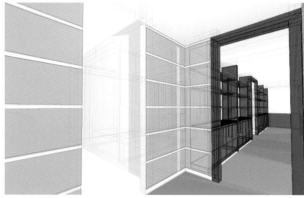

View of living area millwork from entry foyer

View of living area millwork

Island storage was proposed in place of the removed wall. To round out the symmetry, a complementary "entertainment island" was installed where the TV is located. It is hidden when not in use, but emerges from within on demand via a custom-built, swiveling lift mechanism.

The furniture layout, with bar seating at the island, a dining table and chandelier on axis with the bedroom doors, the sofa nested against the back wall, and an open area in the center, created a clear "kitchen-dining-den-living" arrangement within the loft-like open space.

The master bedroom entry was moved from its original location near the front foyer to the center of the enlarged living room. Low cabinetry and upper shelving flanks the doorway, to replace the lost window-seat storage, providing a strong central axis.

In stark contrast with the bright white master bathroom, the powder room has darker colors reflected on the fully mirrored walls. The wide plank porcelain flooring turns up to become the glass "disappearing" basin´s backsplash.

Credits

Alexander Butler, Principal & Founder
Alexander Butler | Design Services, LLC
www.abdsnyc.com
General contractor: Jordan Design Group
www.jordandg.com

Appliances and Materials

Carpeting: Patterson Flynn Martin, and Edward Fields
Countertops & Backsplash: Caesarstone "Raven" at all Formica cabinets and Caesarstone "Pure White" at kitchen and entertainment islands
Floors: "Ginza" wood look porcelain floor tile and "Glassos" 24" x 24" tile in master bathroom
Furniture: Holly Hunt, BB Italia, Poliform,

Ligne Roset, and Design Within Reach
Millwork: "Smokey Brown Pear" Formica laminate, matte finish at kitchen, shelving, frames, doors, and radiator covers; shop-sprayed paint, satin finish at islands and in bathrooms
Plumbing Fixtures: Ginger "Surface" sink and bathroom fixtures, Axor "Starck" and "Citterio" fixtures in showers, Robern "Uplift" medicine

cabinets throughout
Sinks: "Ladena" by Kohler at master bathroom, "Aquagrande" by Lacava at guest bathroom, and "4500G Block Crystal" by Lacava at powder room
Walls: Painted sheetrock, "Noblesse" wall-covering from Weitzner behind shelving and around column in living room; high-gloss European lacquer over MDF panels in foyer

CONTEMPORARY LOFT

1,480 sq. ft.

Washington, District of Columbia, United States

STUDIO SANTALLA

Photos © Geoffrey Hodgdon

ERNESTO
SANTALLA

Architecture
Interior Architecture
Furniture
Graphics

Designer: Ernesto Santalla

www.ernestosantalla.com

> PROVIDE A GALLERY-LIKE SETTING FOR THE DISPLAY OF WALL ART AND SCULPTURES

> DEVISE A DESIGN THAT HIGHLIGHTS THE WAREHOUSE ORIGINS OF THE BUILDING

A FORMER CAR DEALERSHIP WAS INTEGRATED INTO A NEW RESIDENTIAL BUILDING AS PART OF THE REVITALIZATION OF WASHINGTON, DC'S 14TH STREET, KNOWN AS "AUTO ROW" BACK IN THE 1950s.

"The conversion of an industrial loft space into a condominium apartment capitalized on hype and focused less on the uniqueness of the space. Loft spaces, or true loft spaces, are rare in DC because of building height restrictions and a greater demand for traditional architecture.

"If there is a thing loft spaces have in common, it's openness. They present the opportunity to contrast raw finished elements. Open ceilings with exposed structures are often the norm, too. We were fortunate to be selected to remodel this apartment and to bring out its true potential, while creating a setting for the display of great artwork.

"The clients preferred a sparse, streamlined look, so we eliminated baseboards throughout and concealed wires and switches wherever possible. Custom, built-in cabinets float on the walls at both ends of the apartment (the office and bedroom).

"The clients—a childless couple—didn't want a lot of private space, so we removed the wall that had separated the bedroom and replaced it with a floating partition that doesn't reach the ceiling.

"The clients wanted to make it special. We explored its full potential and decided to reconnect it with its warehouse origins."

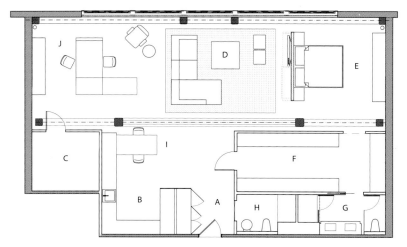

New floor plan

A. Entry hall
B. Kitchen
C. Mechanical room
D. Living area
E. Bedroom

F. Walk-in closet
G. Master bathroom
H. Bathroom
I. Dining area
J. Home office

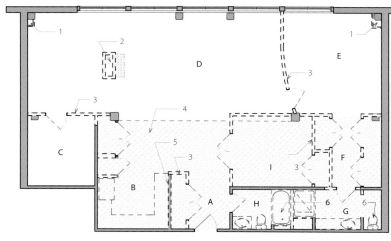

Demolition plan

A. Entry hall
B. Kitchen
C. Mechanical room
D. Living/dining area
E. Bedroom

F. Walk-in closet
G. Master bathroom
H. Bathroom
I. Den

1. Remove plasterboard to expose pipe
2. Remove fireplace completely
3. Remove partition
4. Remove ceiling in hatched area
5. Lower wall
6. Remove all fixtures

The space was gutted, the ceilings were exposed, and the mechanical systems redirected wherever possible to convey a sense of openness. Drains and ducts were incorporated into the design. The idea was to make the space look like we had done nothing to it. In its current iteration, the loft is basically one large room, encompassing the living, home office, and kitchen areas.

Detailing throughout reflects an industrial aesthetic. Extra-heavy doors hang flush with the walls to create a sense of visual continuity. Extensive track lighting maximizes the effect of the art, and old-growth hickory floors with eight-inch planks have a satin finish that reveals the wood's imperfections, adding an element of texture and contrast.

The custom kitchen features
stainless-steel Miele wall appliances.
A nook below a Kirindongo sculpture
accommodates a dining table from
the clients' previous home that's
been trimmed to fit the space. It can
be pulled out for company.

Facing the living area, a sliding panel on the freestanding wall displays a painting by French-born artist Philippe Zanolino. When open, it reveals the TV and when closed, it showcases a painting, which complements a second piece by the same artist.

Santalla describes the bedroom as "an intimate space where you can still feel the amplitude of the apartment." Another Zanolino piece hangs over the bed. Opposite, Keith Milow paintings on aluminum sheets hang above a floating cabinet.

An adjacent den was replaced by a large master bath and walk-in closet with a floor-to-ceiling, semi-custom elfa shelf system. The bath is tiled in porcelain and boasts a long vanity, where Kohler sinks and fittings are illuminated by Viabizzuno lighting.

Credits

Architect: Ernesto Santalla
www.ernestosantalla.com

Appliances and Materials

Appliances: Miele
Artwork: Keith Millow, Philippe Zanolino, Yubi Kirindongo, and Nelson Carrillho
Bathroom walls: Porcelain tile
Bathroom sinks and fittings: Kohler
Floors: Old-growth hickory, satin finished
Lighting: Viabizzuno Lighting
Walk-in closet shelving: elfa

PREWAR UPPER EAST SIDE RENOVATION

1,300 sq. ft.

New York, New York, United States

KANE ARCHITECTURE AND URBAN DESIGN

Photos © Devon Banks

Designer: Ted Kane,
architect and interior designer

www.kane-aud.com

> OPEN UP THE KITCHEN TO PROVIDE A BETTER CONNECTION WITH THE LIVING SPACES AND TO CREATE A LESS FORMAL EATING AREA FOR BREAKFAST AND AFTERNOON KIDS' HOMEWORK

> EXPAND A FORMER MAID'S ROOM INTO A THIRD BEDROOM SO THAT EACH CHILD CAN HAVE HIS OWN ROOM

> CREATE A SECOND FULL BATHROOM

> MODERNIZE THE EXISTING BATHROOM AND KITCHEN WITH NEW FINISHES AND FIXTURES

> REPLACE ALL ELECTRICAL AND PLUMBING SYSTEMS

THE APARTMENT IS LOCATED ON THE FOURTH FLOOR OF A NINE-STORY PREWAR BUILDING BUILT IN 1915 ON THE UPPER EAST SIDE IN MANHATTAN. THE PREVIOUS OWNER HAD OCCUPIED THE UNIT FOR MORE THAN FIFTY YEARS AND IT HAD ONLY BEEN MINIMALLY UPDATED DURING THAT TIME.

"One of the challenges that the apartment presented was that its original layout included an enclosed kitchen and maid's room, which were separated from the rest of the apartment. They were linked directly to a service entrance, which was common for buildings of this era. The apartment also had only one bathroom and no laundry room.

"The design sought to modernize and open the apartment through subtle transformations and removals, while maintaining the prewar character. The job included removing the walls separating the kitchen from the entry foyer, the foyer from the living room, and the living room from the kitchen to create a continuous flow of space.

"An existing building drainpipe was found within the wall separating the kitchen from the living room. Since the pipe could not be removed, it was wrapped by a built-in bookcase, which in turn linked the living area and the kitchen. Another challenge was to squeeze a second bathroom into what were an existing very small washroom and an adjacent utility closet. These were combined to provide a compact yet full second bathroom. Since the unit is on a lower floor and faces a rear courtyard, day lighting was scarce. To improve this situation, the wood floors were sanded and lightened. The walls and ceilings received a fresh coat of paint to help reflect light deeper into the apartment."

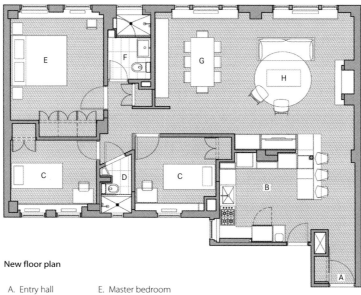

New floor plan

A. Entry hall   E. Master bedroom
B. Kitchen   F. Master bathroom
C. Bedroom   G. Dining area
D. Bathroom   H. Living area

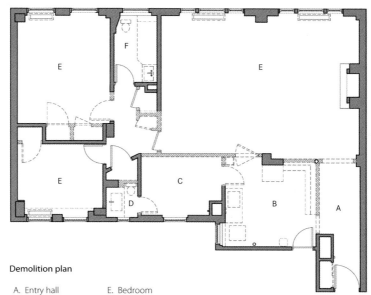

Demolition plan

A. Entry hall   E. Bedroom
B. Kitchen   F. Bathroom
C. Maid's room   G. Living/dining area
D. Powder room

Tall cabinets combining closed and open shelving make up for the lack of wall space for storage, while providing some degree of separation between functions. New built-ins below the window sills throughout the apartment hide the radiators and mechanical equipment and provide additional storage.

A wall was removed at the entry hallway to open up the kitchen and provide a small breakfast counter. From the hallway, the kitchen and living room are connected by full height millwork. While the kitchen retained its original footprint, storage was expanded by replacing an existing doorway to the former maid's room with full height pantry shelving.

The original bathroom was reconfigured to provide a walk-in shower and additional storage. A floating sink with storage makes the narrow space feel larger. Integrated custom cabinetry hides the mechanical equipment and a simple pendant illuminates the ceiling and brightens the interior-facing bedroom.

Credits

**Architect: Kane Architecture and
Urban Design**
www.kane-aud.com

**General contractor: Rafal Smola /
Taurus Construction**
www.taurusconstructioninc.com

Appliances and Materials

Appliances: Miele oven, Wolf cooktop,
and Fisher & Paykel dishwasher
Bathroom faucet:
California Faucets
Bathroom medecine cabinet:
Duravit
Bathroom sink: Duravit
Floors: Red oak
Kitchen backsplash: "Carrara" porce-
lain tile from Stone Source

Kitchen countertops: "Glacier White",
Corian solid surfaces
Kitchen sink and faucet: "Purist"
by Kohler
Lighting: "Talo" wall sconce by
Artemide (living area), PH5 by Louis
Poulsen (dining area)
Walls: "Chantilly Lace" by
Benjamin Moore

CHIADO APARTMENT

1,292 sq. ft.

Lisbon, Portugal

FALA ATELIER

Photos © Fernando Guerra/FG+SG

Design team: Filipe Magalhães, Ana Luisa Soares, Ahmend Belkhodja, and Ana Lima

www.falaatelier.com

> PRESERVE AS MANY ARCHITECTURAL FEATURES AS POSSIBLE

> INCORPORATE ORIGINAL STRUCTURAL ELEMENTS INTO THE DESIGN

> CREATE A CLEAR DISTINCTION BETWEEN PUBLIC AND PRIVATE REALMS

THE REDESIGN OF THIS OLD APARTMENT EMPHASIZES GEOMETRY AND COLOR USING AN ARTISTIC APPROACH THAT IS REMINISCENT OF PAPER-CUT COLLAGES.

"Built at the turn of the nineteenth century, the apartment presented a fragmented arrangement of rooms and an erratic—almost negligent—overlay of successive interventions by previous owners who ignored the original character of the space. The client wanted a coherent space organization and the old plaster ceilings to be preserved.

"The project was as much a restoration as it was a new design. On the one hand, we wanted to enhance the architectural features of the apartment, and on the other, we wanted to correct the mistakes of past remodels—which we thought obscured these architectural elements.

"As we corrected the past mistakes, night and day zones became clear. We proposed a single wall, half-circular in shape, to achieve this separation. The living area became an open plan composed of three clearly defined zones: living area, dining area, and kitchen. A difference in floor height and the use of different flooring materials made the distinction between these different zones even clearer. The living area—like the entry hall and the bedrooms—has Portuguese pine flooring, the dining area—and the bathrooms—has a raised floor finished in micro cement, and the kitchen has a decorative mosaic tile floor that harmonizes with the geometric and colorful motifs used throughout the apartment."

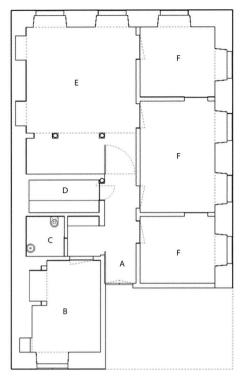

Existing floor plan

A. Entry hall   D. Pantry
B. Kitchen   E. Living/dining room
C. Bathroom   F. Bedroom

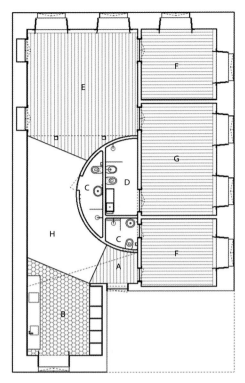

New floor plan

A. Entry hall   E. Living area
B. Kitchen   F. Bedroom
C. Bathroom   G. Master bedroom
D. Master bathroom H. Dining area

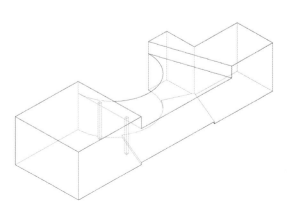

Spatial diagram

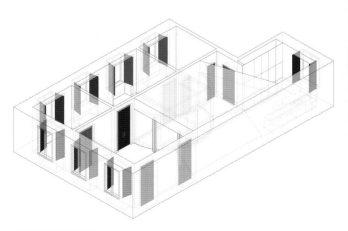

Color scheme diagram

280

The minimalist color palette and material selection highlight the clear yet powerful geometry of the apartment's layout. The tall old doors and shutters are painted in three different shades of blue, complementing the colorful furnishings. The overall design provides the apartment with a distinctive character.

Modern furnishings, bold colors, and graphic elements offset the original solid architecture.

Credits

Architect: Fala Atelier
www.falaatelier.com

**General contractor and structural
engineer: João Carrasco**

Appliances and Materials

Appliances: Smeg
Cabinetry: By local millwork shop
Countertop: Brushed aluminum
Floors: Mosaic, Portuguese pine,
microcement
Kitchen: Steel cabinets, lacquered in
anthracite gray
Sink and faucet: Bruma
Walls: Farrow & Ball paint and micro-
cement

HARRISON AVENUE APARTMENT

1,250 sq. ft.

Boston, Massachusetts, United States

———

OVER,UNDER

Photos © Bob O'Connor

Design team: **Chris Grimley,** architect and **Kelly Smith,** interior designer. Both are also owners of the apartment.

www.overcommaunder.com

> INCREASE STORAGE CAPACITY OF BEDROOMS, LIVING ROOM, KITCHEN, AND BATHROOM

> CREATE MORE COUNTER SPACE IN THE KITCHEN AND TAKE ADVANTAGE OF UNDERUTILIZED SPACE

> OPEN UP KITCHEN TO DINING AREA

CHRIS GRIMLEY OF BOSTON-BASED ARCHITECTURE FIRM OVER, UN-DER PUT HIS DESIGN CHOPS TO THE TEST AND REMODELED HIS OWN HOME WITH THE HELP OF HIS WIFE, KELLY SMITH.

"We purchased our South End apartment under Boston's first-time afford-able homebuyer's program at a time when we were both starting design businesses—an architecture and design studio, over, under, and a felt design and distribution company, filzfelt.

"The existing apartment design had many awkward corners and sequences that weren't amenable to additional storage for the family, which was exact-ly what we needed. Initially, we decided to undertake the remodel step by step, planned over a long time frame. We cut openings in walls, removed all the carpet, and painted the floors with garage paint. At that point, we were still faced with a two-bedroom apartment and a growing family. The birth of our first child sped things up. Around that time, the felt company was acquired by Knoll. These two events fast-tracked the design and its imple-mentation.

"The design brings into play a series of perpendicular walls that hold various items: cabinets in the bedroom and living room, linen drawers adjacent to the bathroom, and an entry nook. The kitchen was completely overhauled to take advantage of underutilized space and gain more counter surface. But the best design decision we made was opening the kitchen up to the dining room. Everything else then fell easily into place: We removed a built-in pantry and replaced it with a new one, reclaimed from the closets in the second bedroom.

"We were fortunate to have a friend and general contractor who oversaw the project. We did most of the demolition ourselves, and subcontractors were coordinated directly by over,under. All that kept the costs of the reno-vation down."

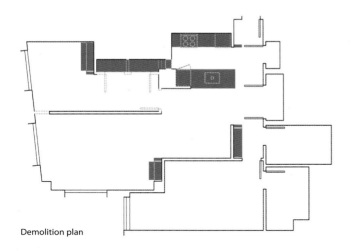

Demolition plan

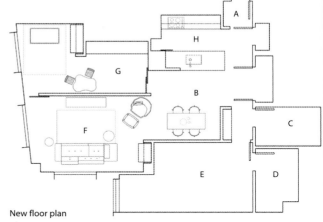

New floor plan

A. Entry
B. Dining area
C. Bathroom
D. Closet

E. Master bedroom
F. Living area
G. Children's bedroom
H. Kitchen

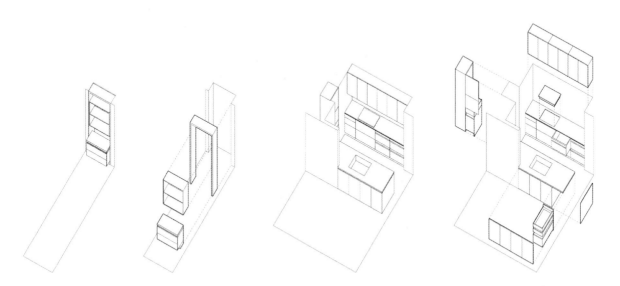

Axonometric views of cabinets

Sliding doors replaced the more conventional swing doors to favor of a modern living space where circulation flows effortlessly. In the new design walls don't work strictly as enclosures but as elements that frame different areas.

The existing full refrigerator
was replaced by under-counter
appliances. That allowed the upper
cabinets to run the full length of the
kitchen, and more counter space was
gained for food preparation.

The entry nook serves to prevent
views to the kitchen from the front
door, a common and disappointing
design strategy for many
condominiums.

A neutral color palette was used throughout the apartment to create a sense of continuity and homogeneity. This neutral backdrop was perfect for the creation of focal points, visually demarcating different areas.

Credits

Architect: over,under
www.overcommaunder.com

General contractor: FKIA
www.studiofkia.com

Appliances and Materials

Appliances: Sub-Zero, Wolf, and Bosch
Cabinets: Sharp woodworking
Countertop and backsplash: Formica solid surface
Floors: Epoxy
Furniture and fixtures: Knoll, Vitra, Flos, Tom Dixon, Libratone, Rich Brilliant Willing

Kitchen: MDF with catalyzed paint
Sink and faucet: Kohler
Walls: Paint and felt by Filzfelt

WEISEL APARTMENT

1,184 sq. ft.

Tel Aviv, Israel

___

DORI INTERIOR DESIGN
Photos © Adi Cohen Zedek

Designer: Dori Redlich

www.dori-design.com

> DEVISE A SPACIOUS LIVING AREA THAT
> INCORPORATES A DINING AREA AN OPEN
> KITCHEN

> OPEN UP ENCLOSED TERRACE

> TRANSFORM BEDROOM AT THE BACK OF THE
> APARTMENT INTO A LARGE PRIVATE MASTER
> BEDROOM

> PROVIDE A HOME OFFICE THAT CAN BE PART
> OF THE LIVING SPACE BUT ALSO CAN BE
> SEPARATED

THE NEW DESIGN BY DORI INTERIOR DESIGN CLEARED UP THIS APARTMENT'S INTERIOR AND OPENED IT UP TO THE STREET.

"We found an apartment comprised of piecemeal rooms along a narrow, dark corridor. The kitchen was tiny, enclosed, and inconveniently positioned far from the living and dining room. The apartment was originally designed to have front and back terraces, but previous owners, who preferred to incorporate these outdoor spaces into their interior living spaces, had blocked them. With these outdoor spaces totally closed off, the apartment received little natural light and was poorly ventilated.

"The renovation process took about three and a half months in order to give back to the apartment its original character and make it fit for the client and his family.

"The location in the heart of Tel Aviv and a peculiar *mashrabiya*-like screen at the front wall facing the boulevard originated our design concept, which we titled 'When Urban and Ethnic Styles Meet.' The *mashrabiya* is an architectural element typical of Islamic architecture. It was widely used in urban areas and was meant to separate interior and exterior spaces, allow for light and ventilation, and provide some degree of privacy.

"The design maximizes natural lighting and openness, avoiding obtrusive partitions. Separation of spaces is only used where strictly necessary. In this respect, the need for storage space and for room separation was resolved with one single custom-made piece of cabinetry that makes a splash the moment one steps into the apartment."

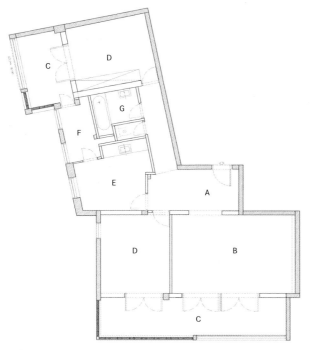

Existing floor plan

A. Entry hall
B. Living/dining room
C. Enclosed terrace
D. Bedroom
E. Kitchen
F. Service room
G. Bathroom

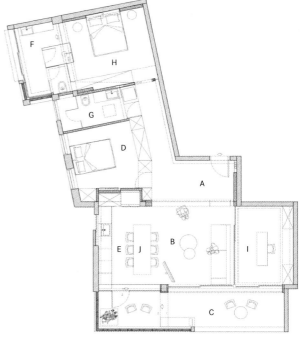

New floor plan

A. Entry hall
B. Living area
C. Enclosed terrace
D. Bedroom
E. Kitchen
F. Master bathroom
G. Bathroom
H. Master bedroom
I. Home office
J. Dining area

To achieve the goals set by the client, the apartment layout needed to be reassessed. The reconfiguration of the apartment started with a clean slate, eliminating the excess hallways and vestibules. New plumbing, electrical, and air-conditioning systems provide for an efficient and comfortable living environment.

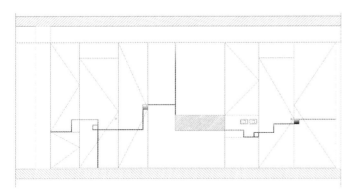

Elevation at wall cabinetry

The once dreary hallway was transformed into a pleasant wood-clad passage that connects the public areas at the front of the apartment to the private master bedroom at the back.

A curtain can be drawn along the glass partition for further separation. This design is in response to the desire to keep the separation between areas to a minimum. A minimalist shelving system delimits the entry hall while allowing visual connection with the living area and through the windows beyond.

The spacious living area is functional and allows for different seating arrangements, which promotes socializing.

In this apartment, shutters were hiding the *mashrabiya*, but in other apartments in the building, the mashrabiya panels had been permanently walled in. The design gives this element its original function back, creating a secluded semi-outdoor space on two levels, a perfect book-wine-scotch-friendly nook.

A floor-to-ceiling glass partition
with a curtain separates the master
bedroom and the en suite where the
shower takes center stage.

Credits

Architect: Dori Interior Design
www.dori-design.com

**General contractor: Shai Oda and
Motaz Aodi**

Appliances and Materials

Home accessories: Ferm Living and
Normann Copenhagen
Lighting: Asaf Weinbroom
Tile work: Patricia Urquiola for Mutina

BONDI APARTMENT

1,175 sq. ft.

Sydney, New South Wales, Australia

MCK ARCHITECTS

Photos © Douglas Frost

Design team: Mark Cashman, architect and
Rowena Marsh, architect

www.mckarchitects.com

> REMOVE WALLS TO OPEN UP THE SPACE

> OPEN UP KITCHEN TO THE COURTYARD

> EXTEND EXISTING COURTYARD TO INCLUDE
   OUTDOOR SHOWER

> REFURBISH EXISTING LAUNDRY ROOM AND
   INSTALL A SECOND TOILET IN IT

> RETAIN SOME ART DECO FEATURES ORIGINAL
   TO THE APARTMENT

THE CLIENTS CALL THE APARTMENT THEIR "DIAMOND IN THE SKY." THEY WERE USED TO LIVING BY THE WATER, BUT DUE TO WORK AND THE KIDS' SCHOOLING, THEY FOUND THEMSELVES SPENDING MORE TIME IN THE CITY.

"The clients hail from New Zealand and South Africa and wanted the re-model to reflect their cultures. The apartment is on the rooftop of an Art Deco building. As it is Heritage-listed, we had to submit a report for council approval before we started any work. The council did impose some restrictions: We had to retain the decorative cornices and external corbels and no changes could be made to windows and exterior doors.

"The apartment had brick walls, and a traditional timber floor (whitewashed at some point), and showed signs of some modern changes in the kitchen and bathroom that might have taken place during the 1980s. The courtyard was tired, with terra-cotta tiles and no seating. Despite the deteriorated conditions, the apartment and the courtyard had some original Art Deco features worth preserving to maintain its original character and acknowledge the history of the building. At the same time, we wanted to open up the apartment for modern living.

"The removal of walls that divided the space was key to achieving our goal. Then we inserted a new joinery wall to provide spaces with different functions. The materials were picked to create a space that was elegant and modern, but most importantly, conducive to relaxation."

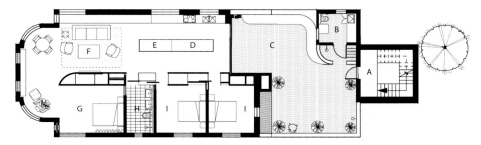

New floor plan

A. Entry staircase   F. Living area
B. Laundry room   G. Master bedroom
C. Courtyard   H. Bathroom
D. Kitchen   I. Bedroom
E. Dining area

Existing floor plan

A. Entry staircase   F. Living room
B. Laundry room   G. Sun room
C. Courtyard   H. Master bedroom
D. Kitchen   I. Bathroom
E. Dining room   J. Bedroom

Longitudinal section

A new sliding bifold door opens up the entire width of the kitchen to the courtyard, allowing this area to become primary living space during the summer.

The new seat and extension of the laundry help to define the exterior courtyard space and tie it back to the internal spaces. It gives the outdoor space its own identity and purpose. The new curved seating provides an entertainment space. Its design takes its cue from the Art Deco building and the overall material palette.

A long kitchen bench runs the length of the space, linking the kitchen, dining, and living areas physically and visually.

The timber combined with the black-and-white color scheme ties all the spaces together. This clean yet powerful scheme is a reflection of both the clients' and MCK's design sensibilities.

A built-up wall running the entire length of the apartment has doors that differentiate the open public living area from the bedrooms. It also contains storage and cabinetry serving both areas.

The minimalist palette was intended to make the whole apartment feel unified. The cornice wraps around the entire area, and is only broken up by the joinery dividing the apartment into public and private spaces.

The built-up wall is short of the front of the apartment with a projecting bay. Like the round corners of the bay, the wall end curves as if avoiding the bay. This allowed to keep that end of the apartment open. the bedroom is merely enclosed at that end with a light curtain to let light in from the bay's windows.

Credits

Architect: MCK ARCHITECTS
www.mckarchitects.com

Builder: Laycock Constructions

Joinery: Scarelli

Structural Engineer: SDA Structures
www.sdastructures.com.au

Surveyor: Eric Scerri & Associates

Appliances and Materials

Appliances: Miele, Fisher & Paykel, Qasair, and Vintec
Countertop: Solid Surface, "Bright White" by Staron; stainless steel; and recycled French oak
Fixtures: Astra Walker and Robert Plumb
Floors: Parquetry, blackbutt timber decking
Furniture: Hans Wegner, Eames,

Bang & Olufsen, Poltrona Frau, and Spence & Lyda
Joinery: Polyurethane, 30% gloss in "natural white" by Dulux; and oak veneer
Tiles: "Backgammon" concrete tile by Popham Design
Walls: Paint (internally), acrylic render (externally); "Lexicon Half" by Dulux

QUEEN STREET APARTMENT

1,173 sq. ft.

Auckland, New Zealand

DORRINGTON ATCHESON ARCHITECTS

Photos © Emma-Jane Hetherington

Design team: **Tim Dorrington**, architect and
Marie-Claire Henderson, project architect

www.daa.co.nz

> CONVERT A WAREHOUSE FORMERLY USED
  TO STORE PAINTINGS INTO A HOME FOR THE
  OWNER AND HER TWO DAUGHTERS

> FIT A TIGHTLY PLANNED PROGRAM INTO THE
  SPACE AVAILABLE

> GAIN NATURAL LIGHTING FROM WINDOWS
  ON TWO WALLS INTO THE CORE OF THE
  APARTMENT

> TAKE ADVANTAGE OF THE HIGH CEILING TO
  INSERT A NEW STRUCTURE THAT EXPANDS
  THE USABLE SQUARE FOOTAGE OF THE
  APARTMENT

DORRINGTON ATCHESON ARCHITECTS TRANSFORMED A FORMER PAINTING STORAGE SPACE IN A HERITAGE BUILDING INTO A HOME FOR A FAMILY MOVING FROM A SUBURBAN TO AN URBAN LOCATION.

"This apartment occupies the second floor of the Endeans Building, a prominent edifice on Auckland's waterfront, built in the early twentieth century. It was once used to store paintings from a nearby gallery. In converting the space into a home for the owner and her two daughters, we had to comply with the requirements of the Auckland City Council and liaise with the Historic Places Trust.

"The Endeans was the first Auckland example of a multi-story building that used a steel-reinforced concrete system of construction. It was converted to a mixed-use residential and commercial property in 1993 and enjoys an urban aspect with views of the Britomart Transport Centre.

"There was no opportunity to alter the dimensions of the envelope, so the challenges were to fit a tightly planned program into the footprint and to gain enough light into the core of the apartment from windows on two sides. Positive attributes were its high ceilings and a selection of industrial materials. Together, they provide the apartment with a sense of loftiness.

"We designed a contemporary insertion clad in black steel, which was slotted into the empty volume to act as bedrooms for the children.

"The owners, who moved from a typical suburban home, are enjoying their city-centered outlook and a new way of living."

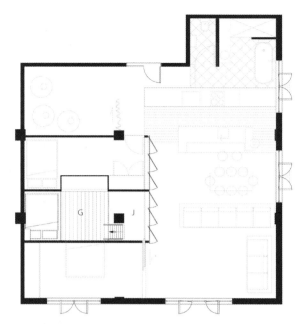

New mezzanine plan

A. Entry hall
B. Bathroom
C. Kitchen
D. Dining area
E. Living area
F. Master bedroom
G. Bedroom
H. Master bathroom
I. Bedroom
J. Open to below

New floor plan

An overall black-and-white scheme ties in features of the Edwardian original style and the contemporary industrial look. Textural contrast is captured in the interior palette: roughness in the concrete floors and columns; smoothness in the clear powder-coated steel.

High clerestory windows allow light to enter the insertion and vertical steel-bladed curtain walls can be opened for accessibility to the space. The kitchen is backed by a similar spine of steel that shields the main bathroom behind.

One room was built as a mezzanine
so that an en suite for the master
bedroom could slot beneath it.

The double-height cube, at only six-and-a-half feet wide, was divided into two—a room for each girl—then furnished with built-in beds and desks.

Credits

Architect: Dorrington Atcheson Architects
www.daa.co.nz

Appliances and Materials

Appliances: Fisher & Paykel
Doors: Reclaimed old stable doors to main bedroom from Mantells Mt Eden
Floors: Concrete, recycled and stained matai (timber) in the kitchen, and tiles in the bathroom and en suite
Furniture and fixtures: French wine funnel down lights over the dining table by Flotsam and Jetsam; sofa by Forma; mirror in the living room by Acland Holdings; red-top side table by Kartell; red cubes from ECC
Kitchen backsplash: Antique mirrors by Eric Knoben
Kitchen cabinetry: 0.6 mm steel (clear powder-coated)
Kitchen countertop: Glass-reinforced concrete
Kitchen faucet: "Livello" by KWC

Kitchen sink: Contemporary medium bowl by Valoré
Walls: Paint and clear powder-coated black steel

PETROLEUM APARTMENT

968 sq. ft.

São Paulo, Brazil

DIEGO REVOLLO ARQUITETURA
Photos © Alain Brugier

Designer: Diego Revollo

www.diegorevollo.com.br

> TRANSLATE THE CLIENT'S AESTHETIC
  INTERESTS INTO AN ADEQUATE
  ARCHITECTURAL LANGUAGE

> EXPAND THE LIVING AREA BY ELIMINATING
  ONE OF THE EXISTING ROOMS

> OPEN UP THE KITCHEN TO THE LIVING AREA

> RECONFIGURE THE AREA FORMERLY
  OCCUPIED BY THE MAID'S BEDROOM AND
  BATHROOM TO MAKE ROOM FOR A HOME
  OFFICE OPEN TO THE LIVING AREA

> THE COLOR SCHEME EMPHASIZES THE USE
  OF "PETROLEUM BLUE" TO EXPRESS THE
  CLIENT'S LOVE FOR THE SEA AND THE COLORS
  BLUE AND GREEN

DIEGO REVOLLO RENOVATED AN OVERLY-FRAGMENTED APARTMENT TO ADAPT IT TO THE NEEDS OF ITS NEW OWNER: A SINGLE YOUNG MAN WHO IS AN ART AND PHOTOGRAPHY ENTHUSIAST.

"When I first met the client, the referential images he showed me weren't of rooms or furniture. Instead, they depicted his own aesthetic universe: his love for the ocean, for blue and green, and even more specifically, for petroleum blue. These premises set the tone for the vibrant décor of the apartment. But before we got into the aesthetics of the place, there were some spatial issues that needed to be resolved in the new plan. The apartment felt cramped, not so much for the lack of space, but for the inefficiency of the layout and its inability to satisfy the spatial needs of the new owner.

"We expanded the living area by eliminating one of the bedrooms and by incorporating a new open kitchen into it. The block that was formerly occupied by the maid's room and a small impractical bathroom off the laundry room was obstructing the flow between different areas. This block was completely reconfigured, which allowed us to use that space in a way that would better respond to the needs of the owner. We managed to fit a new powder room, enlarge the master bathroom, and make room for a small home office corner that is open to the living area. With the new plan, the spaces flowed much better.

"Cabinetry details became more obvious to us as we got the plan resolved and began to introduce design elements that reflected the aesthetic taste of the client: light gray ceilings and warm light wood floors complemented the white walls with accents of petroleum blue. The furniture selection gave the overall design a slight retro look."

A. Elevator
B. Entry hall
C. Balcony
D. Living area
E. Dressing room
F. Bedroom
G. Master bathroom
H. Bathroom
I. Home office
J. Powder room
K. Laundry room
L. Kitchen
M. Dining area

New floor plan

A. Elevator
B. Living/dining area
C. Balcony
D. Bedroom
E. Vestibule
F. Master bedroom
G. Master bathroom
H. Bathroom
I. Maid's room
J. Powder room
K. Laundry room
L. Kitchen

Existing floor plan

The apartment is accessed by the keyed elevator, opening directly into the open plan living area.

The kitchen is an integral part of the living area. It is modern and inviting, in line with the overall design of the apartment.

Light gray walls and ceilings, a honey-colored wood floor, and wall paneling combine with the vigorous accent color that gives this project its name: Petroleum Blue.

The master suite is located away from the living area, giving the owner a comfortable retreat with a private bathroom and dressing room.

The décor is simple, yet unconventional.
In the bathroom, the vanities look
more like sinks on top of dressers.

Credits

Architect:
Diego Revollo Arquitetura
www.diegorevollo.com.br

Appliances and Materials

Bathroom: Mirrors by Vidroart; tableware and metals by Construdomus; counter in Caesarstone "Deep Ocean"; cabinet design by Diego Revollo Arquitetura and fabrication by Marcenaria Inovart; floor in Tauari wood by Gasômetro; and hexagonal tiles "Sixties Gray" by Decortiles
Bedroom: headboard and bed-side tables by Diego Revollo Arquitetura

Kitchen: Floors and walls clad in hexagonal "Beaufort M6256" by Atlas; cabinets in Tauari wood; kitchen design by Todeschini; island counter in Caesarstone "Oyster"; and glass door by Vidroart
Office, dining, and living areas: Cabinetry by Marcenaria Inovart

OVERLAP

960 sq. ft.

Taoyuan, Taiwan

GANNA DESIGN
Photos © MWphotoinc / Siew Shien Sam

Design team: Shih-Jie Lin and Ting-Liang Chen

www.ganna-design.com

> PROVIDE A LARGE PIECE OF CABINETRY FOR
> THE DISPLAY OF THE OWNERS' TOYS AND
> MINIATURES COLLECTION, AND THE OBJECTS
> PURCHASED DURING THEIR TRIPS

> PROVIDE STORAGE

> DEVISE MULTIFUNCTIONAL SPACES AND
> FURNITURE TO MAKE THE MOST OF THE
> SPACE AVAILABLE

A COUPLE OF COLLECTORS HAVE THEIR NEW HOME REDONE TO SAT-ISFY THEIR NEED TO STORE AND DISPLAY THEIR TOYS AND TRINKETS.

"He likes to collect toys and miniatures; she likes to collect knickknacks brought from their travels. Needless to say, shelving space for the display of their items was at the top of their whish list. The two owners also wanted their home to have a relaxed atmosphere. These two simple requirements guided a design that stands out for its geometric composition of horizontal pieces of millwork. What at the beginning might have been a project focused on the creation of cabinets and shelving where collectibles can be organized and displayed, became a design exercise for the organization of the space.

"At the entry lobby, a floating bench along one side extends toward the main space to become a platform that serves as seating at the dining table. The opposite wall has a shelf that turns into a kitchen island. Taking center stage in the main space is a long display case, which is just as long as the dining table. With the platform along one side and additional seating on the other side, the long table allows for various simultaneous activities to take place.

"The living area isn't particularly spacious, but two large panels slide and stack against a third fixed wood wall to expand its area and transform the space to satisfy different spatial needs."

A. Entry hall
B. Living/dining area
C. Children's bedroom
D. Master bedroom
E. Master bathroom
F. Bathroom
G. Balcony
H. Kitchen

New floor plan

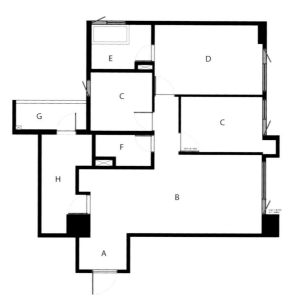

A. Entry hall
B. Living/dining room
C. Bedroom
D. Master bedroom
E. Master bathroom
F. Bathroom
G. Balcony
H. Kitchen

Existing floor plan

The horizontality of the millwork marks the circulation path throughout the apartment, linking one space with the next.

A long display cabinet is the
centerpiece of the living area.

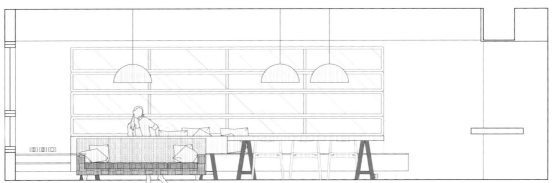

Elevation at display case

The layout of the apartment makes the most of the available space, providing movable partitions that transform it according to spatial needs.

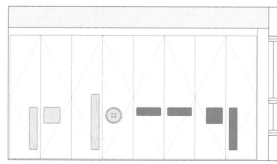

Elevation at bedroom closet

Throughout the apartment,
furnishings and cabinetry details
were inspired by the owners'
collection of toys and miniatures.

Credits

Interior designer and general contractor: Ganna Design
www.ganna-design.com

Appliances and Materials

Floors: Wood
Walls: White paint with back accents
Kitchen cabinets and countertops: Melamine
Cabinetry: Melamine cabinets
Furniture and fixtures: "Nextmaruni" armless chair by SANAA for Maruni, "FL/Y" pendants from Kartell, "Shuffle

MH1" side table by Mia Hamborg, "Baxter" dining chairs, and Shangrila sofa from Macromaison

GALLERY LOFT APARTMENT

958 sq. ft.

Tel Aviv, Israel

BLV DESIGN/ARCHITECTURE

Photos © Amit Geron, Ilan Nachum, and
BLV Design/Architecture

Designer: **Zohar BenLavie**, architect

www.blv.co.il

> CREATE A MODERN AND SPACIOUS LAYOUT
  TO SATISFY THE NEEDS OF A YOUNG FAMILY

> INCREASE USABLE AREA, STORAGE CAPACITY,
  AND PROPERTY VALUE

THIS APARTMENT IS LOCATED IN THE YOUNG AND VIBRANT "SOHO" AREA OF TEL AVIV, IN A HISTORIC BUILDING BUILT IN 1934.

"The apartment was a one-bedroom and one-bathroom, but potentially could be reorganized to suit the needs of a young couple starting a family. They wanted a place with a spacious living area, comfortable for day-to-day activities as well as for entertaining.

"To achieve the goals of the renovation, we decided to take advantage of the apartment's high ceilings to add a 237-square-foot mezzanine. An existing central structural beam gave us an indication as to how far the new floor could extend. The new steel structure was thin enough that it would not generate a confined space under the new floor.

"We wanted the place to project an open lifestyle that promoted interaction. So we opened the kitchen to face the living and dining area and by doing so, not only did we incorporate the kitchen into the social area, but also we amplified the perception of overall space.

"The new mezzanine also took care of the lack of storage, providing closets and cabinets that expanded the apartment's capacity for storage, while adding visual interest."

New floor plan

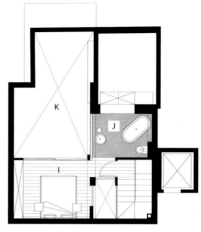

New mezzanine plan

A. Entry hall
B. Home office
C. Bathroom and washer/dryer
D. Bedroom
E. Terrace
F. Dining area
G. Living area
H. Eat-in kitchen
I. Master bedroom
J. Master bathroom
K. Open to below

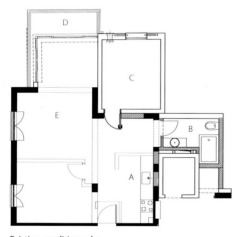

Existing conditions plan

A. Kitchen
B. Bathroom
C. Bedroom
D. Terrace
E. Living/dining room

The existing floor plan was reconfigured to accommodate a compact but efficient kitchen, a spacious living and dining area, a bedroom, a bathroom, and a home office. The new mezzanine provided room for the master bedroom, a full bathroom, and generous storage space. A screen separates the home office from the entry, creating a sense of demarcation, while allowing visual connection with the space beyond.

Not only did the new mezzanine increase the area of usable space, but it also enhanced the spatial experience of the apartment, creating exciting physical and visual relationships between the two levels.

The lack of storage was approached creatively, providing modern pieces of cabinetry such as the built-in piece in the living area. The bookcase provides open and closed shelving.

A sense of spaciousness is achieved through glass enclosures that allow visual connection between the two levels of the apartment.

Floor-to-ceiling sliding glass panels behind a glass guardrail allow for full visual connection and air flow, while pleated shades control light and privacy levels.

The extensive use of glass allows light
to reach the deepest corners of the
apartment and enhances the spatial
experience.

Credits

**Architect: Zohar BenLavie/
BLV Design|Architecture**
www.blv.co.il

Carpenter: Hibel & Sons Carpenter
www.greenbuttonsolutions.com/hibel

Curtain and blinds: Las Cortinas
www.cortinas.co.il

Engineer: Hadar Porat

**General contractor:
Meir Sharf Construction**
www.meirsharf.com

Glass work: Hamarha
www.hamarha.co.il

Metalwork: Ram Rosenberg

Appliances and Materials

Artwork: Hayah Sheps Avtalion and
Naomi Fuks
Bathroom floor: Herringbone bluestone
mosaic, Aloni
Bathroom sink: Vitreous china
Bathroom walls: Porcelain tiles, Aloni
Bathtub: Resin stone by ElGal
Bedroom floor: Natural oak planks
Faucets: Colorado Series by ElGal
Furniture and fixtures: Vibia, ICone,

Tollman's, Elemento, ID Design, Beitili,
PickUp, TEMA, Urbanik, Tzemer
Kitchen: Formica
Kitchen counter: Caesarstone

ART AND LIGHT

920 sq. ft.

New York, New York, United States

ANDREW MIKHAEL ARCHITECT

Photos © Brad Dickson

Designer: **Andrew Mikhael**, architect

www.andrewmikhael.com

> CREATE A GALLERY SETTING FOR THE
  DISPLAY OF ARTWORK

> ENHANCE THE LIVING AREA TO ENCOURAGE
  GATHERINGS

> ENLARGE THE BATHROOMS WITHOUT
  SACRIFICING SOCIAL SPACE

THIS APARTMENT'S REMODEL EMPHASIZES ART AND LIGHT IN A
SETTING DEVISED TO ACCOMMODATE THE OWNERS' AFFINITY FOR
ENTERTAINING.

"Our clients, two lawyers and their toddler, wanted to renovate their apartment, but more specifically, they wanted to enhance their living spaces.
They also wanted a place where they could display their art collection in a
gallery setting that would make a splash when they hosted their frequent
parties.

"The overall idea behind the renovation was to create a fun and inspiring
home for entertaining and relaxing in a clean design environment. We
shaped the lighting to be an abstract object that moves through the apartment. In the case of the kitchen and hallway, the client can also change the
mood of the space with a push of a button, washing walls in color. Lighting
as object continues into the living area, providing illumination and sparkle
without taking up an inch of floor space. We changed the layouts of the
bathrooms from awkward leftover space to generous and accommodating.
Our clients preferred social space over bedrooms, and so we reduced the
bedroom space in favor of a wider living room. Extra large panels slide open
to combine the bedrooms and the living area into one space."

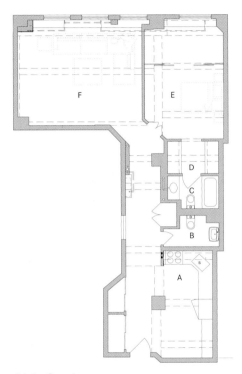

Existing floor plan

A. Kitchen
B. Powder room
C. Master bathroom
D. Walk-through closet
E. Bedroom
F. Living area

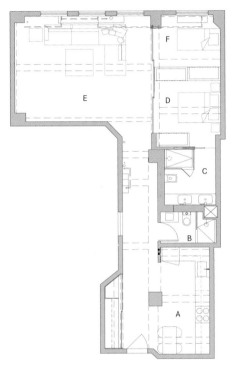

New floor plan

A. Kitchen
B. Bathroom
C. Master bathroom
D. Master bedroom
E. Living area
F. Bedroom

A dark glass block window in the hallway was converted into an art installation of light. With its multiple settings, one can rotate through a selection of colors to wash the space in colored light, instantly changing the mood and feel of the space.

House parties are a regular event here and inspired many design decisions. The front door opens directly into the kitchen—the center of party action. The geometric composition of the cabinets complement the colorful art while the LED lighting enhances this playful layout and sets the mood for the entire apartment.

The bedroom is enclosed by large scale sliding doors, which double as art walls. These movable walls may be closed for privacy while entertaining guests and opened to integrate the bedroom and living room into one open space.

Anchored from the doorway, both the angular vanity of folding Corian and walnut and the vanity light in the guest bathroom point their energy inward. The hallway light portal glows lime green in the background. The master bathroom (opposite) is expanded from a tight space to a minimalist black-and-white square room.

Credits

Architect: Andrew Mikhael Architect
www.andrewmikhael.com

Appliances and Materials

Appliances: Viking range, Miele hood, Sub-Zero fridge, Bosch dishwasher
Bathroom fixtures: Fantini, Duravit, and Infinity Drain (blue bathroom); Dornbracht, Laufen, Ceramica Cielo, Robern, and Infinity Drain (master bedroom)
Bathroom tiles: Mosa and Artistic Tile (master bedroom), Mosa (blue bathroom)

Custom cabinets and vanities: Integrated sink by Corian (blue bathroom and kitchen); back-painted glass in the kitchen
Floors: Wide-plank white oak floor by Carlisle
Kitchen faucet: Vola
Lighting: Controllable LED lights (kitchen and hallway); "Truline" (hallway and living area) by Pure Light,

Sonneman (blue bathroom and kitchen); Alma Light (master bedroom)
Walls: Benjamin Moore paint

POTTS POINT APARTMENT

904 sq. ft.

Sydney, New South Wales, Australia

TFAD

Photos © Tom Ferguson

Designer: Tom Ferguson

www.tfad.com.au

> RELOCATE THE KITCHEN TO A MORE CENTRAL
  POSITION, AND OPEN IT TO THE LIVING AREA

> ENSURE THAT THE DESIGN OF THE NEW
  KITCHEN BLENDS WITH THE REST OF THE
  OPEN SPACE

> MAINTAIN THE ORIGINAL ART DECO
  FEATURES, INCLUDING CORNICES AND
  ARCHITRAVES

THE REDESIGN OF THIS APARTMENT MIXES HISTORIC ARCHITEC-
TURAL DETAILING WITH MODERN DECOR FOR A COZY AND UNIQUE
HOME INTERIOR.

"The project was for the renovation of a 1930s apartment in Potts Point, Sydney. The apartment is at the rear of the building and has views of the Sydney skyline from the northern and western side windows. It was in relatively original condition with intact decorative ceilings. The bathroom, while intact, was in poor condition.

"The project was thoroughly planned using knowledge of the building gained from renovations to other apartments, so there were no real unexpected challenges. Some of the design difficulties included the design of a new kitchen bench to be more furniture-like so that the main room wouldn't feel like it was dominated by the kitchen. Also, wall removal had to be made structurally possible."

Demolition plan

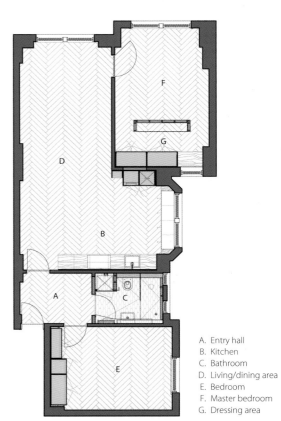

New floor plan

A. Entry hall
B. Kitchen
C. Bathroom
D. Living/dining room
E. Bedroom

1. Remove section of wall for new door
2. Remove section of wall
3. Remove door leaf, frame, and architrave. Retain existing leaf (and architraves, if possible)
4. Line of beams
5. Strip out bathroom, including tiles, fittings, and fixtures
6. Remove plasterboard niches
7. Remove kitchen cabinetry

A. Entry hall
B. Kitchen
C. Bathroom
D. Living/dining area
E. Bedroom
F. Master bedroom
G. Dressing area

The apartment was in its original configuration, which consisted of two bedrooms both on the western side. There was an entry hall, a central living room with a northern window, a small original bathroom, and a large kitchen at the front of the apartment, also with a northern window.

Across from the kitchen's work counter, a tall cabinet conceals the refrigerator. It has open shelves at one side and across the top, providing space for books within reach of the window seat. This gives the kitchen a more living-room–like feel, which is further explored through the use of simple yet elegant materials and finishes.

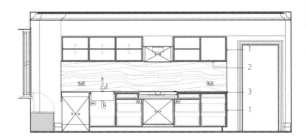

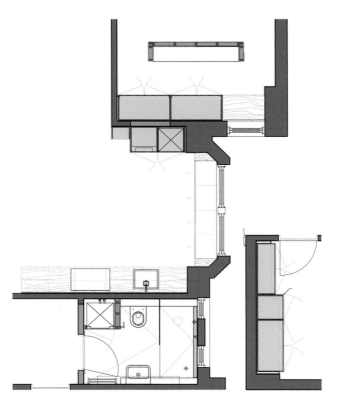

Kitchen detail plan

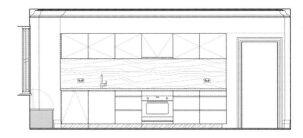

Kitchen elevations

1. Polyurethane finished side panel
2. Polyurethane finished soffit with LED strip
3. Brass edge detail to side

The plumbing for both the bathroom and the kitchen had to be resolved so that it could connect into the building's existing external plumbing risers. This was done by placing the new kitchen against the wall backing onto the bathroom and incorporating a plinth in the bathroom to conceal drainage pipes.

A room divider functions as the headboard on the bedroom side and as shelving on the dressing area side to accommodate an easily accessible walk-in closet.

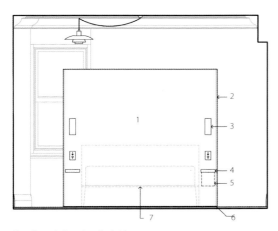

Headboard elevation. Bed side

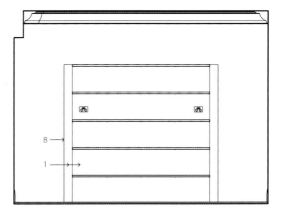

Headboard elevation. Dressing area side

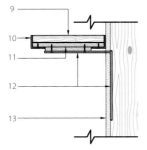

Bedside table detail

1. Wallpaper
2. Radius corner
3. Recessed trimless light
4. Cantilevered table
5. Concealed fixing to framing
6. Shadow line detail to base
7. Outline of bed
8. Plasterboard or MDF surround wall
9. Pietra Gray marble
10. Brass angle
11. 2 plywood sheets, 1 as base for marble, 1 for fixing to angle
12. Stainless steel angle bracket
13. Plasterboard installed after bracket, concealing bracket

Credits

Architect: TFAD
www.tfad.com.au

Appliances and Materials

Architraves: Finger joint pine. Profile to match existing
Bathroom ceiling: Dulux Wash & Wear, Kitchen & Bathroom Ceiling Flat
Bedroon headboard: Wallpaper
Bedroom shelving: MDF shelves, two-pak polyurethane paint, 10% matte finish
Floor: Tongue-and-groove parquet, European oak, Penza (color), Grande (format), Osmo Hardwax Oil finish
General ceilings: Dulux Ceiling White throughout
Kitchen backsplash: Pietra Gray marble, honed and clear sealed
Kitchen cabinetry: MDF cabinets, two-pak polyurethane paint, "Black Caviar" 10% matte finish
Kitchen countertops: Pietra Gray marble, honed and clear sealed, with brass edge
Skirting: Finger joint pine. Profile to match existing
Trim: Dulux Aquanamel, semigloss finish
Walls: Dulux Wash & Wear, low sheen finish

FORMER CARETAKER'S APARTMENT

800 sq. ft.

São Paulo, Brazil

ABPA ARQUITETURA
Photos © Ana Mello

Design team: André Becker Pennewaert,
architect; **Marinha Martins**, project manager;
and Rafael Boaretto, intern
www.abpa.arq.br

> OPEN UP THE ENTIRE INTERIOR

> MAINTAIN THE INTEGRITY OF THE ORIGINAL
  STRUCTURE

> MAXIMIZE THE AVAILABLE SPACE

> TAKE ADVANTAGE OF THE INCREASED
  CEILING HEIGHT AFTER THE REMOVAL OF THE
  SUSPENDED PLASTER FINISH

THE REFURBISHMENT OF A FORMER CARETAKER'S APARTMENT IN A
1960s BUILDING IN DOWNTOWN SÃO PAULO GIVES THE NEW HOME
AMPLE LIVING SPACES AND PANORAMIC VIEWS.

"The building's structure is all standard concrete construction, but the caretaker's apartment is a different story. It is a separate smaller structure with a
square footprint that sits on the building's rooftop. The exterior brick walls
support an old wood and ceramic tiled roof.

"Inside, what seemed like a concrete slab was in fact a nonstructural stucco
ceiling. Also, none of the interior partitions were structural. These existing
conditions allowed us to gut the whole interior and start with a clean slate.
The removal of the stucco ceiling revealed a wooden roof structure that was
intact and in good condition. It was so beautiful that we decided to incorporate it into our design as a key element. With this extra height, the apartment
acquired different proportions that expanded the perception of the space.

"The original square plan, which had been divided into five cramped and
very dark rooms, became an expansive open space. This new situation led
us to develop a design concept that would incorporate new architectural
elements without interfering with the integrity of the original space. This
resulted in the insertion of a simple wooden box that takes up half the floor
area of the apartment to accommodate some of the functions of the new
home. The top of the box is short of the tie beams and is accessible, providing additional space for storage or occasional sleepovers."

View of building's urban context

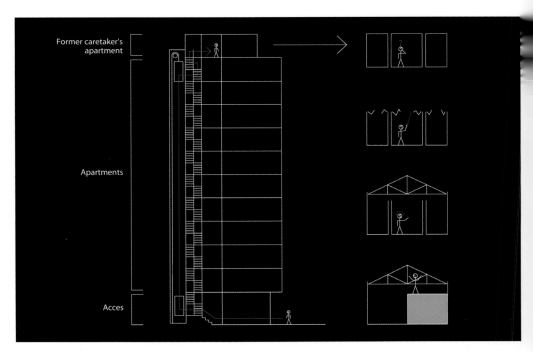

Former caretaker's apartment

Apartments

Acces

Without direct elevator access—
it stops one floor below—the
apartment is reached via one flight
of stairs.

Building section and remodel strategy diagram

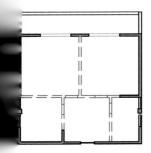

Demolition plan

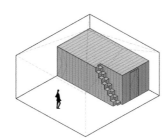

Conceptual diagram

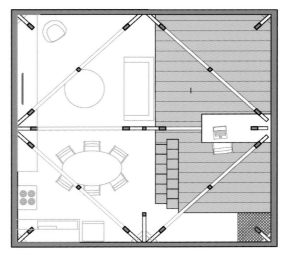

New mezzanine floor plan

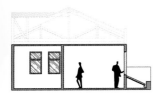

Sections. Before, during and after
construction

Section through new terrace,
living area, and laundry closet

Section through new living area
and bedroom

Section through new bathroom
and kitchen

New main floor plan

A. Entry   F. Living area
B. Laundry closet   G. Dining area
C. Bathroom   H. Kitchen
D. Bedroom   I. Mezzanine
E. Terrace

The newly exposed roof structure revealed new design opportunities, such as the possibility of adding a mezzanine level.

The private areas, such as the bedroom and bathroom, are contained inside a large wooden volume, along with cabinets, stairs, and the mezzanine on top, which accommodates a desk.

Despite the fact that the space
is compact, not only does the
apartment not feel cramped, but
it is also fitted with all the comforts
that a home needs.

The wall closest to the street is set back from the building's façade (because the caretaker's house could not designed to be visible from the street). A steeply sloped ceramic tile roof extended from the original windowsills to the building's front wall. The project changed this roof into a flat wooden deck above it, creating a new terrace facing the city.

Credits

Architect: ABPA Architecture
www.abpa.arq.br

**General contractor: Valter Torres /
Torres e Miranda**

**Structural engineer: Eduardo Duprat /
Benedictis**
www.benedictis.com.br

Lighting consultant: Reka Iluminação
www.reka.com.br

Woodworking: ArtMoveis Marcenaria
www.marcenariaartmoveis.com

Appliances and Materials

Cabinets and carpentry: Naval
hardboard
Countertop and sink: Stainless steel
by Mekal
Floors: Perobinha wood (throughout),
dry shake concrete (bathroom)
Furniture and fixtures: Couch from
Marché Art de Vie, Green table from
dpot, Panton chair, Eames DSR chair,
and Saarinen Tulip wood table

Roof: Ceramic tiles over wood structure
Walls: Dry shake concrete

TRAMA

753 sq. ft.

Brazilia, Brazil

SEMERENE ARQUITETURA INTERIOR

Photos © Joana França

Designer: Clarice Semerene

www.semerene.com

> OPTIMIZE THE USE OF THE APARTMENT'S LIMITED SPACE

> CREATE A FLEXIBLE OPEN SPACE THAT CAN ACCOMMODATE DIFFERENT SCENARIOS

> CREATE A DESIGN THAT REFLECTS THE PERSONALITY OF THE APARTMENT'S OWNERS

THE APARTMENT, LOCATED IN A RECENTLY CONSTRUCTED BUILDING, WAS DESIGNED TO MEET THE NEEDS OF A YOUNG COUPLE AND THEIR FAST-PACED LIFESTYLES.

"Originally, the apartment had a conventional layout of clearly separated rooms, including a living room, kitchen, laundry room, two bedrooms, and a bathroom.

"The new design addresses the clients' need for a living environment with fewer partitions, fluid circulation, and multipurpose spaces that can adapt to different scenarios of everyday life. The physical barriers between areas of different functions were eliminated in favor of an open plan with a central element that organizes the living area while fulfilling various functions. It consists of a metal shelf, a kitchen island, and a long dining table. This ensemble is the heart of the home.

"The functions of the kitchen are reduced to the bare essentials and are organized along a wall adjacent to the central island. Opposite, a wall formed by a set of sliding wood panels allows the main space to spill into a room that can serve as home office and guest room.

"We chose neutral and natural materials such as concrete and wood, with accents of bright lively colors that add zest to the décor. The result is a lively home where the couple can relax and recharge."

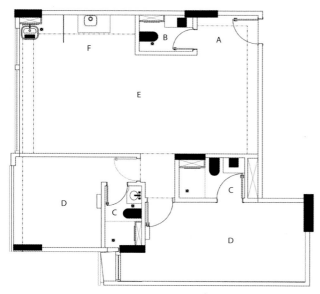

Existing floor plan

A. Entry
B. Powder room
C. Bathroom
D. Bedroom
E. Living/dining area
F. Kitchen

New floor plan

A. Entry
B. Walk-in closet
C. Bathroom
D. Master bedroom
E. Living area
F. Kitchen
G. Dining area
H. Home office

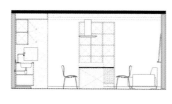

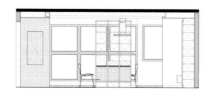

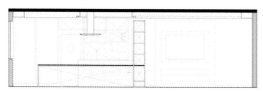

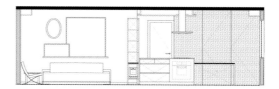

Elevations at living, dining, and kitchen areas

With the new layout, the different areas merge with each other. The use of color also contributes to the clarity of the different areas. A bright blue wall in the living area reflects the dynamic lifestyle of the apartment's occupants.

The design of the metal open shelf
is inspired by the towering buildings
in Brazilia.

The metal shelf anchors the new design to the existing space. As part of a central composition, it organizes the different areas without obstructing sight lines. Aesthetically, it brings an industrial element to the décor of the apartment.

Splashes of color animate a
predominantly neutral palette.

Credits

Interior designer:
Semerene Arquitetura Interior
www.semerene.com

Collaborator:
Fernanda Abreu

Appliances and Materials

Concrete, wood, metal, and vibrant
paint colors

MIDTOWN WEST

720 sq. ft.

New York, New York, United States

GENERAL ASSEMBLY

Photos © Devin Banks

Designer: Sarah Lawlor Zames

www.genassembly.com

> OPEN UP KITCHEN TO DINING AREA

> COME UP WITH A STORAGE SYSTEM THAT
  CAN SERVE BOTH THE LIVING AREA AND
  THE KITCHEN, AND AT THE SAME TIME BE
  VISUALLY APPEALING.

THIS ONE-BEDROOM APARTMENT GOT A AIRY MAKEOVER WITH CLEVER MILLWORK IDEAS.

"The apartment had fantastic views of the city skyline that weren't viewable from the closed-off galley kitchen. The goal of the renovation was simple: to open up the space and modernize it, while providing as much storage space and functionality as possible in a reduced space. The project was completed in a very tight time frame. The entire construction process took only about a month. The space was a small one to work in, and being an older building, we did encounter some plumbing surprises. Luckily we had a good contractor on board and were able to solve problems as they came up. The end result is an open space with millwork that integrates into the surrounding living spaces."

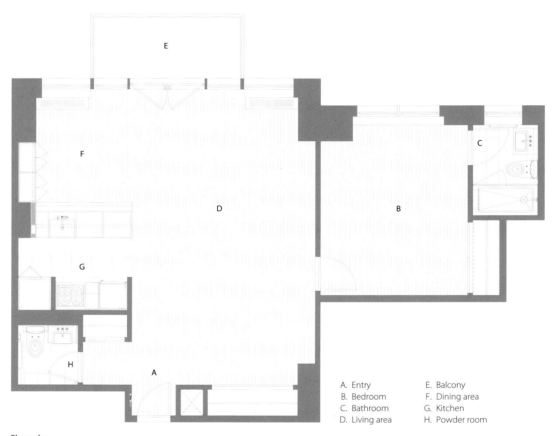

E

F

D

B

C

G

A

H

A. Entry   E. Balcony
B. Bedroom   F. Dining area
C. Bathroom   G. Kitchen
D. Living area   H. Powder room

Floor plan

Credits

Designer: General Assembly
www.genassembly.com

General contractor: Ecostruct
www.ecostruct.com

Millwork: DHWWD
www.dhwwd.com

Appliances and Materials

Cabinets: Sapele wood
Countertops: Caesarstone
Lighting: Crown Minor by Nemo Lighting
Tiles: Ann Sacks

RF HOME

700 sq. ft.

Rio de Janeiro, Brazil

___

STUDIO RO+CA

Photos © Denilson Machado and Studio RO+CA

Design team: Rodrigo Beze, Carlos Carvalho, and Caio Carvalho, architects

www.studioroca.com.br

> INCORPORATE THE KITCHEN INTO THE LIVING AREA

> CREATE AN OPEN PLAN THAT CAN ACCOMMODATE SMALL GATHERINGS

> CREATE FLUID SPACES THAT MERGE TOGETHER

> USE A COLOR PALETTE TO PROVIDE THE APARTMENT WITH LIGHT AND POSITIVE ENERGY

THIS SMALL APARTMENT GETS A FRESH AND BRIGHT UPLIFT TO REFLECT THE DYNAMIC LIFESTYLE OF ITS NEW OCCUPANTS.

"The apartment was a new build with an industrial look. With a contained plan, it wasn't fit for the owner's outgoing lifestyle. We were hired to transform this fragmented space into an open plan that could accommodate small gatherings.

"The main idea behind the design concept was to create more open and exciting spaces. In keeping with this idea, the kitchen was incorporated into the living room, forming one single open space. The selection of materials and finishes was aimed at creating fluid and integrated areas, while providing a sense of warmth. The furniture, the decoration, and the artwork reflect the personality of the owner."

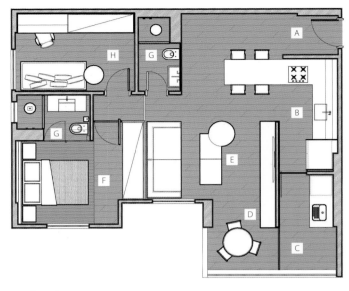

New floor plan

A. Entry hall
B. Kitchen
C. Laundry room
D. Dining area
E. Living area
F. Bedroom
G. Bathroom
H. Office

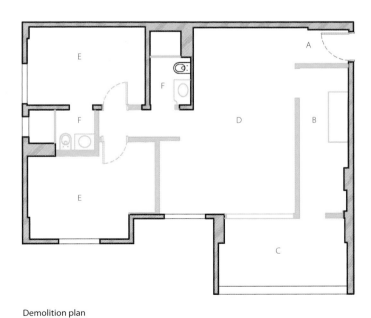

The interior of the apartment was almost entirely gutted to improve the organization of the spaces. The new plan also encloses a former terrace to increase the interior floor area

Demolition plan

A. Entry hall
B. Kitchen
C. Terrace
D. Living/dining room
E. Bedroom
F. Bathroom

The original terrace is incorporated into the living area to create a bright breakfast nook. This simple alteration in the layout is a significant improvement in the way the space is used, making it more pleasant and flexible with better connections between different areas.

To provide the apartment with a special and distinctive touch, different materials were mixed, including pinewood wall paneling, whitewashed brick walls, and paint that creates the rich textural look of polished concrete.

By replacing a solid wall with a frosted glass partition and sliding door, the master bathroom gains a few inches of valuable space. The glass allows light to pass through while providing privacy.

Credits

Architect: Studio RO+CA
www.studioroca.com.br

Appliances and Materials

Appliances: Brastemp
Carpeting: Phenicia Tapetes Persas
Floors: Florin
Furniture and fixtures: LZ Studio,
Arquivo Contemporâneo, Way Design
Kitchen: Florense
Walls: Passeio Revestimentos

EFFICIENT LIVING

600 sq. ft.

Washington, District of Columbia, United States

—

ERNESTO SANTALLA

Photos © Geoffrey Hodgdon

ERNESTO
SANTALLA

Architecture
Interior Architecture
Furniture
Graphics

Designer: Ernesto Santalla

www.ernestosantalla.com

> GUT A DATED ONE-BEDROOM APARTMENT
AND RECONFIGURE ITS INTERIOR FOR
EFFICIENT LIVING IN A SMALL SPACE

THIS APARTMENT SERVES AS A PIED-À-TERRE TO AN ATTORNEY
WHO ALTERNATES BETWEEN CITIES. THE CLIENT'S DESIRED USE OF
THE SPACE WAS KEY TO THE DESIGN SOLUTION.

"Small spaces tend to be claustrophobic and dark, and this apartment fit that
description. To fix the problem, most walls and doors were removed, mini-
mizing the feeling of constraint and maximizing natural lighting. The apartment was organized to enhance functionality, openness. The former kitchen
was turned into a multipurpose zone for informal dining, display shelving,
and overflow space for the home office. All are spatial considerations that
are often neglected in large spaces, but are significant in small ones.

"Every element in the space is both functional and architectural. Full-height
cabinetry enhances the elevation of the space, which at times was only
slightly higher than the minimum code requirements because of existing
ductwork and sprinkler lines. In the living area, which doubles as work space,
built-in cabinetry optimizes the use of a party wall, while providing visual
interest. The simplification of design elements, coupled with an architectural
use of color, lighting, and materials, alleviate the formerly confined space,
while large pieces of artwork occupy key focal points."

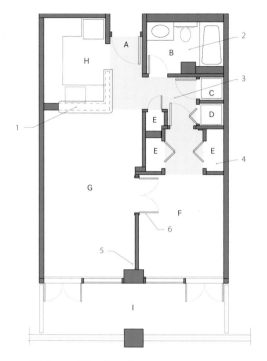

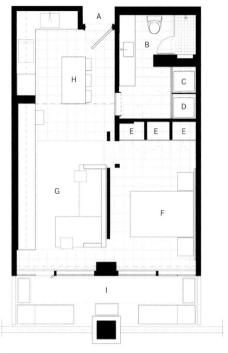

Existing conditions floor plan

A. Entry
B. Bathroom
C. Washer/dryer
D. Mechanical room
E. Closet

F. Bedroom
G. Living/dining room
H. Kitchen
I. Terrace

1. Wall creates separation from rest of space
2. Small, dark, and cramped bathroom
3. Excessive circulation
4. Small closets
5. Full height wall blocks light
6. Double door limits usable space

New floor plan

A. Entry
B. Bathroom
C. Washer/dryer
D. Mechanical room
E. Closet

F. Bedroom
G. Living area
H. Kitchen/dining area
I. Terrace

In a very small apartment, where every square inch counts, the existing space had an excessive amount of circulation room, as indicated by the shaded areas. The kitchen, albeit open, was separated from the main living space by a low wall. A full-height wall enclosed the bedroom, making yet another small, cramped room.

The new layout of the apartment provides an unobstructed main space front to back, with built-ins along the perimeter walls to maximize open space. With walls on three sides and a guardrail on the other, the balcony is very much a "room" that extends the interior to the exterior.

Combining spaces and functions created a much larger bathroom. The sleeping area is both open to and separate from the main space. The "soft" enclosure expands former tight and narrow spaces.

Credits

Architect: Ernesto Santalla
www.ernestosantalla.com

Appliances and Materials

Modern lines, neutral colors, and an
upscale collection of paintings and
sculpture
Cabinetry: Anigre wood
Countertop: Caesarstone

EAST VILLAGE STUDIO

475 sq. ft.

New York, New York, United States

ETELAMAKI ARCHITECTURE

Photos © Mikiko Kikuyama

Designer: Jeff Etelamaki, Principal

www.etelamakiarchitecture.com

> CREATE A SENSE OF AMPLITUDE DESPITE THE
  REDUCED DIMENSIONS OF THE APARTMENT

> MAKE THE MOST OF THE AVAILABLE SPACE
  TO OPTIMIZE FUNCTIONALITY

> CREATE A DISTINCT, SEMI-PRIVATE
  SLEEPING AREA

A YOUNG NEWLYWED COUPLE HAD PURCHASED THIS HOME WITH THE IDEA IN MIND TO TURN IT INTO A SOPHISTICATED, "GROWN UP" VERSION OF A MANHATTAN STUDIO.

"The client's primary concern was that the design should accommodate their shared guilty pleasure: television. Ideally, there would be a TV in both the living and sleeping areas.

"All existing partitions were removed to create a single, open living space. A separate, partitioned bedroom, a 'sleeping pod,' was incorporated into the space to maintain the open feel. The issue was how to provide some level of privacy. This was resolved by the creation of a walnut screen, which dematerializes and minimizes the visual impact of the volume. The sleeping pod was raised to give it a sense of separation from the rest of the apartment. The area below was converted into storage compartments, and built-in cabinetry was utilized throughout to make the most efficient use of the space."

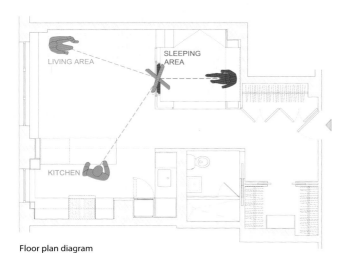

Floor plan diagram

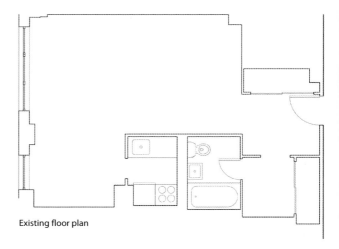

New floor plan

A. Entry hall   D. Eat-in kitchen
B. Walk-in closet   E. Living area
C. Bathroom   F. Bedroom

Existing floor plan

The configuration of this small studio
apartment was developed around the
central position of the TV screen. This
led to the creation of a wooden-slat
structure with a revolving platform
for the TV.

Due to the impracticality of two TVs in such a constrained space, a single rotating TV was installed in a central location. The 360-degree rotation of the TV makes it viewable from the living area, the sleeping area, and the kitchen.

Rich, warm materials such as walnut cabinetry and floors, and slab marble countertops and backsplash give the space the level of sophistication the client desired.

The bathroom appears larger than it actually is thanks the the use of white as the predominant color. Light makes the room feel open and airy, while updated fixtures add spark.

Credits

Architect: Etelamaki Architecture
www.etelamakiarchitecture.com

Interior designer: Robin Klein, Antar
Klein Design and Samantha Gold-
man, Handin/Browne Design
www.antarkleindesign.com
www.handinbrowne.com

General contractor: Badillo Design
& Construction
www.badillodesign.com

Appliances and Materials

Appliances: Bertazonni range, Miele
dishwasher, and Liebherr refrigerator
Cabinets: Walnut veneer
Countertops: Statuary marble slab
and Caesarstone in Blizzard
Flooring: Wide-plank walnut from
Carlisle
Paint: Benjamin Moore

Headboard: "Sedan Plush" in gray
flannel from Pollack
Plumbing fixtures: Kohler
Wallpaper: "Bermuda Hemp" in gra-
phite from Philip Jeffries (living room);
Sumi wallpaper in linen and onix from
Zoffany (entry).

CAMINHA APARTMENT

430 sq. ft.

Caminha, Portugal

———

TIAGO DO VALE ARCHITECTS
Photos © João Morgado

Design team: Tiago do Vale, María Cainzos Osinde, Hugo Quintela and Louane Papin

www.tiagodovale.com

> MAINTAIN ORIGINAL LAYOUT

> KEEP COSTS TO A MINIMUM

> EMPHASIZE THE OPEN CHARACTER
OF THE SPACE

> CREATE A FUNCTIONAL LIVING
ENVIRONMENT BY UPGRADING UTILITIES

BUILT IN THE 1980s, THIS APARTMENT WAS IN DIRE NEED OF REFUR-BISHMENT. BOTH ITS UTILITIES AND ORGANIZATION WERE DATED. THE MAIN DESIGN GOAL WAS TO MAKE THE MOST OF ITS SPATIAL POTEN-TIAL, WHILE UPGRADING IT TO CONTEMPORARY LIVING STANDARDS.

"This small apartment by the sea was uninviting due to an unfortunate choice of dark materials and colors, thirty years of intense use, and a cramped, com-partmentalized layout.. The client required an overall upgrade, including fin-ishes, fixtures, and a completely new kitchen, while maintaining the original organization of the apartment. Also, costs had to be kept down.

"Such a clear brief set the tone for a strong concept. We focused our design efforts on enhancing the spatial perception of the apartment and provid-ing good lighting. We opted for a minimalist approach, using white as the predominant color. But the central piece of this project is a blue volume that simultaneously resolves the need for room enclosures and for kitchen cabinetry. This design gesture brings a colorful and unpretentious touch to the whole apartment.

"While the design is clearly minimalist, there is a willingness to display tex-tured surfaces and detailing aimed at animating the spaces, making a clear reference to the origins of the building, and demarcating different areas. This was achieved by maintaining the ceiling moldings and introducing a pat-terned tile floor in the kitchen.

"All in all, the small apartment provides a relaxing experience and is now fit for thirty more years of simple, joyful use."

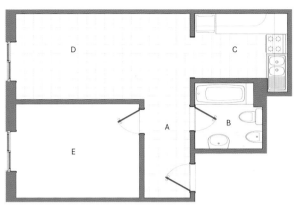

Existing floor plan

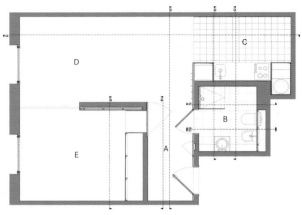

New floor plan

A. Entry hall
B. Bathroom
C. Kitchen
D. Living/dining room
E. Bedroom

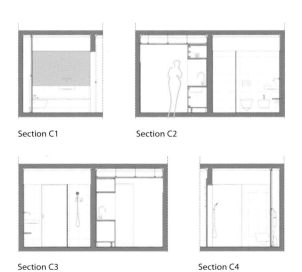

Section C1

Section C2

Section C3

Section C4

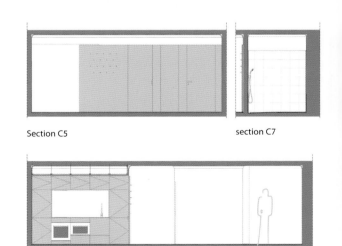

Section C5

section C7

Section C6

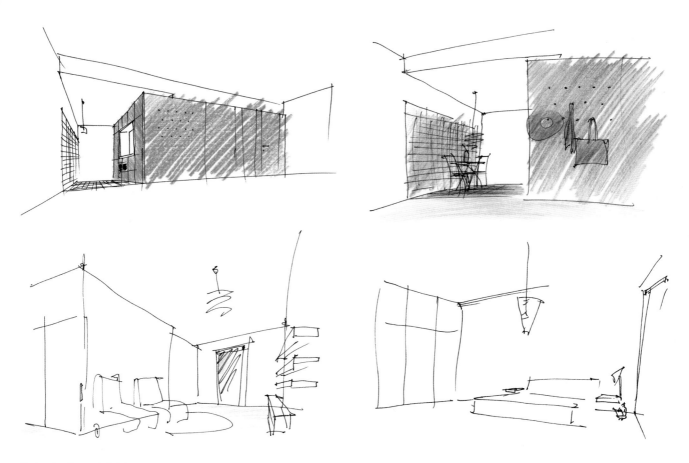

Design development sketches

Blue, the color of the sea, was chosen to finish up the surfaces of the cube, as the apartment is close to the ocean. Regardless of the inspiration, the bright blue volume makes a design statement, while satisfying the owner's desire to keep the original floor plan of the apartment unchanged.

Part of the wall between the living room and the bedroom is a sliding panel. When closed, it allows for a clear separation between the two areas, satisfying the need for privacy. When opened, the two areas fuse into a continuous open space.

The bright blue panels integrate the entry and bathroom doors along one side and then turn the corner to become the kitchen's cabinet fronts. The use of a saturated color, contrasting with the stark white and muted colors, provides the volume with a distinct identity. The space should be understood as a container, into which a distinct object has been inserted.

The blue walls of the kitchen and bathroom volume express the essence of the design concept. The new apartment is conceived as practical, clutter free, and vibrant, reflecting the jovial personality of the dweller.

Credits

Architect: Tiago do Vale Architects
www.tiagodovale.com

General contractor:
Casas do Lima, Limiavez
www.casasdolima.com

Appliances and Materials

Floors: Wood and encaustic cement tiles
Walls: White and blue paint